New Museums
in Spain

Klaus Englert

New Museums in Spain

**with photographs
by Roland Halbe**

Edition Axel Menges

Thanks to everyone who has helped to bring
this book into being, especially the Ministerio
de Cultura in Madrid.

© 2010 Edition Axel Menges, Stuttgart / London
ISBN 978-3-936681-17-8

Prepress: Reinhard Truckenmüller, Stuttgart
Printing and binding: Everbest Printing Co., Ltd.,
China

English translation: Michael Robinson
Editing: Nora Krehl-von Mühlendahl
Design: Axel Menges

Contents

Architectonic attractions

In an article in the daily paper *El País*, the Spanish author Julio Llamazares complains that León in Castile, a town with a population of barely 135 000, boasts a major museum of contemporary art. Llamazares is referring to MUSAC, the Museo de Arte Contemporáneo. This institution was given a spectacular opening in the winter of 2004 and now rivals the major art centres of Madrid and Barcelona: »Not far from the museum, one of the most beautiful cathedrals in Europe, which gets only a few crumbs of the existing culture budget and is funded mainly by donations from private citizens, is struggling to survive. These days there are actually municipalities with a museum of contemporary art, but no hospitals or vital infrastructure. Like medieval cathedrals or 20th century theatres, these museums have become important adverts for cities.«[1]

León demonstrates the decentralised cultural policy which has emerged in Spain over the past two years. The foremost cities – Madrid and Barcelona – do retain their influence, but many smaller cities have been catching up to a considerable extent. León's acquisition of a huge museum for contemporary art and a modern concert hall by the Madrid architects Mansilla + Tuñon plus a modern convention centre by Dominique Perrault within such a short space of time cannot be entirely due to the influence of head of government José Luis Zapatero, who comes from the Castilla y León region himself. The Castilian city is trying to unite potential for progress with its historic heritage, making Llamazares' provocative criticism rather one-sided. The famous Castilian cathedral and university city of Salamanca also wants to be remembered for more than its Roman bridge and its significant architectonic Gothic and Baroque heritage. In 2002, when the city was European Capital of Culture, it therefore converted a former prison which became the Centro de Arte de Salamanca (CASA). The building, which retains its old curtain wall and even some of its cells, was expensively converted using EU funds. This was the first sign of interest in modern art in this city on the Río Tormes, previously home only to a small and unremarkable Art Nouveau museum. Something similar was taking place in the nearby town of Valladolid. The Museo Patio Herreriano, a high-profile museum of Spanish contemporary art housed in a converted convent, was opened there. This temple to the Muses was also built during the economic boom of the millennium, with a media furore surrounding its official opening. It was another project dependent on substantial injections of cash from EU funds. For Castilla y León, a non-industrialised region with an under-performing economy, Spain's entry into the EU in 1986 was an opportunity to invest in culture as well as in vital infrastructure. Unlike many museums located in large cities in Germany, León's MUSAC does not have to worry about running costs – the regional government pays out 5 million euros annually. Two million of this goes to their collection.

Such generosity by the autonomous regions would be unthinkable if the state's coffers were not well-filled. In 2007, Carmen Calvo, then minister for culture, pledged an increase in the museums budget of 38 %. Those museums dependent on public subsidies, at least, profit from this. The prosperity that allows the museum budget to be increased is due to Spain receiving more subsidies from the EU funds than any other member state. According to the most recent figures it will have received 150 billion euros by 2013. Another reason for a boost in growth appeared in the mid-nineties, as massive real estate speculation caused the price of building land to shoot up by a yearly average of 15 %.

To start with it was the museums in large cities that profited most from this – for instance the legendary MACBA in Barcelona, Richard Meier's museum of contemporary art, which still shines like a glowing meteorite in the dark, labyrinthine district of Raval. With a budget of 10.3 million euros, rapidly growing visitor numbers and Barcelona well-maintained profile as a tourist destination, MACBA director Manuel Borja-Villel (who transferred to the renowned Reina Sofía in Madrid in the spring of 2008) must have felt like a Croesus among Spanish museum directors. Finances even allowed him to set up further exhibition spaces in the neighbouring Capella dels Angels, a Gothic chapel dating from 1566. Borja-Villel appreciated the scope he had been granted, but at the same time complained that most of the museums benefiting from the new funds were in major cities and in northern Spain: »Andalusia has a lively scene with many art groups, but no art galleries to match. The money generally goes to the wrong place. In the north, everything is different.«

This imbalance is exemplified by the two monumental museums of contemporary art presently being built on northern Spain's Atlantic coast. When their models were displayed in the legendary New York Museum of Modern Art in an exhibition entitled »On-Site. New Architecture in Spain« in the spring of 2006, they excited international acclaim. This is the Centro de las Artes de A Coruña by the two young architects Victoria Acebo and Ángel Alonso, a duo from Madrid who erected a glass cube directly on the Atlantic, with its two areas, intended for art exhibitions and for dance respectively, separated in an entirely unusual and original construction. Once again, a Madrid team have emerged as Spain's most sought-after museum architects: Luis Mansilla und Emilio Tuñon are presently building the Museo de Cantabria in Santander. This museum is morphologically similar to the MUSAC, with the León museum's unusual light shafts given a more sculptural role. Mansilla + Tuñon designed a cluster of trapezoid prisms reminiscent of the nearby Cantabrian mountain chain. The Museo Provincial de Arqueología y Bellas Artes in Zamora, their much-acclaimed early work, was followed by the Museo de Bellas Artes in Castellón and ultimately by the MUSAC in León. Beside the Museo de Cantabria, they are presently designing the Museo de las Colecciones Reales in Madrid for the Spanish royal family, the Museo de la Automoción in Torrejón de la Calzada in Madrid and the Centro de Artes Visuales – Fundación Helga de Alvear. This project in Cáceres, the provincial capital of Extremadura, involved restoring and extending the Casa Grande to house the extensive collection of contemporary art belonging to Helga de Alvear, a German gallery proprietor living in Madrid. The newest project by Luis Mansilla and Emilio Tuñon is the much acclaimed Museo Territorio de las Migraciones,

which will be located in Algeciras, at the gateway to Africa, and will document the waves of migration from the south. We can only hope that this culture centre will be able to offset the disproportionate endowment of the north's museum scene.

One region of northern Spain which has profited exceptionally from the economic boom while remaining unnoticed by myriads of tourists is the long-underdeveloped district of Galicia. The savings bank Caixa Galicia has built nine culture centres in seven Galician cities, and the Fundación Pedro Barrié de la Maza has also contributed extensively to Galicia's cultural scene. This foundation invited Luis Mansilla and Emilio Tuñon to convert a bank built in 1919 into an art centre. The interest of this new cultural institution lies in the tension between the regal façade and the modern, variable exhibition spaces. Each of the two architects created very different exhibition halls – the »caja mágica« or magic box, whose height can be increased by 4 m means of a floor which can be lowered, a room with a chessboard-like pattern of skylights that let in light whose intensity is constantly changing, and an auditorium whose seating can be lifted up to the ceiling using a single handle. These were devices used by Mansilla + Tuñon to give the restricted available space the maximum adaptability.

Like many other art centres, the MUSAC in León is profiting from a museum boom that has created at least one new centre for modern art every year since the nineties. The northern Spanish regions of Galicia, the Basque Country and rich Catalonia are the main beneficiaries. It was not by accident that the so-called Bilbao effect was first seen on Spain's north coast. In Bilbao in the Basque Country, however, the museum euphoria had a different environment for growth than it did in Castile. While the MUSAC enhanced León and Castile's cultural attractions enduringly, the Museo Guggenheim was built in an unprepossessing city on the Río Nervión – in a cultural void. Since then, Frank O. Gehry's titanium sculpture, confidently straddling the river, has brought culture tourists to Bilbao, who come especially to see his expressive architectonic creation. Bilbao's crowning glory and an economic boon to the community as well, it has created a whole urban infrastructure. Santiago Calatrava built the city's airport and a bridge over the Nervión, then Norman Foster built a modern metro line, and in recent years a hotel complex by Ricardo Legorretas and a neighbouring shopping mall by Robert Stern have followed. In 2007, Arata Isozaki completed two striking high-rise towers alongside Calatrava's bridge. There are more important projects on the banks of the Nervión planned for the future. Rafael Moneo will build a university library, Carlos Ferrater will build two apartment blocks and César Pelli the Torre Iberdrola. The adoptive Londoner Zaha Hadid once again received the most lucrative contract, designing the master plan for Zorrozaurre – a townscape with a disunited appearance on a 57-hectare peninsula at the mouth of the Nervión – and also the EuskoTren headquarters in nearby Durango. Ultimately, the force behind this sudden urban abundance is the mighty New York Gug-genheim Foundation and the tireless Thomas Krens, who is occasionally responsible for motorbike and fashion shows in Museo Guggenheim –

the price the Basques have to pay. The influence of the Guggenheim Bilbao, however, remains immense, and with an annual budget of 27 million euros it is in a different league to most other temples to art.

Many civic politicians now put their faith in the visual impact of their cultural buildings – and all of them, of course, want their own »Guggenheim«. MACBA director Manuel Borja-Villel is critical: »Large, high-profile centres are built simply to create an attractive label. This is one of the problems we have to live with.« In other words: a photogenic, glittering outer shell is no guarantee of outstanding exhibitions, an impressive collection or a good educational program. Loan agreements with their overseas partners oblige major institutions like the Museo Guggenheim and the Museu de les Ciències Príncipe Felipe in Valencia to take on a large proportion of the exhibitions regardless of the content. According to Borja-Villel, these museums profit from their status as crowd-pulling attractions despite their often unattractive exhibition concepts.

Zaragoza is presently enjoying an unprecedented architectural boom. What the 1992 Olympic Games were to Barcelona, EXPO 2008 was to the Aragon city. Francisco Mangado erected the Spanish Pavilion and Zaha Hadid added one more to her numerous Spanish projects – an emblematic bridge-pavilion over the Ebro, a hybrid structure with dynamically constructed lines that pick up on the movement of the river. The Madrid architect team Nieto Sobejano designed the icon of EXPO 2008 – the Congress Palace, which with its sculptural elegance, clear constructive logic and functional flexibility. The Basel firm Herzog & de Meuron were also commissioned to connect the Museo de Zaragoza and the neighbouring Escuela de Arte. The Swiss architects did not restrict themselves to restoring the complex. In fact, they compare their project with the cathedral that Carlos V built within the Great Mosque of Córdoba in the 16th century. On the subject of their concept for four »anchor rooms«, Jacques Herzog and Pierre de Meuron write: »The insertion of the four Anchor Rooms is essentially a violent act because it destroys part of the building, disrupting its historical continuities and spatial configurations. But it is also a liberating act because it opens up a number of new perspectives and adds a number of substantial dimensions to the historicist concept.«[2] The four anchor rooms of the Espacio Goya, which should be completed in 2010, have reconstructions of the Aragon artist's four greatest frescoes – the vault frescoes of Zaragoza's Carthusian monastery of Aula Dei and the Madrid chapel San Antonio de la Florida, and the wall paintings from Goya's private house, Quinta del Sordo and the Real Academia de San Fernando in Madrid. Following the CaixaForum on the Paseo del Prado in Madrid and the Tenerife Espacio de Arte (TEA) in Santa Cruz de Tenerife, this is the Basel architects' third Spanish museum project.

These kinds of projects are a consequence of the Bilbao effect. Since Spanish politicians heard how the Museo Guggenheim has benefited Bilbao's economy, they have been organising restricted-entry competitions between Santiago de Compostela and Málaga. Apart from a few Spanish architects, entrants are exclusively international stars. The Bodega Marqués de Riscal in Elciego

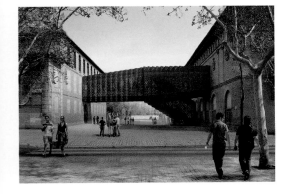

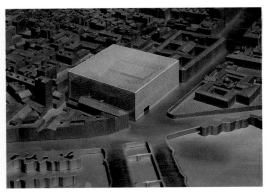

(La Rioja) actually insisted on awarding the contract directly to Frank O. Gehry, who could be expected to produce not only a truly spectacular hotel building, but also a uniquely enticing label. Other stars have also become firmly established in the Spanish architectural scene since the end of the 1990s. They include Norman Foster and Dominique Perrault, but the leading figures are Zaha Hadid, Jean Nouvel and Herzog & de Meuron, who between them win almost every prestigious competition.

Thankfully, the quest for cultural tourism in the south of Spain is able to keep away from gigantism. Richard Gluckman's new Picasso museum in Málaga, situated next to the Arabic Alcazaba and the Roman amphitheatre and integrated beautifully into the fabric of the old town, may have been a great success, but one cannot help asking why Spain is dedicating yet another museum to its great artist, why an international celebrity and media fair had to accompany its official opening in 2003 – and whether the wasted EU money could not have been better spent on building art centres across Andalusia, as proposed by MUSAC dircetor Agustín Pérez-Rubio. Thanks to this cash bonanza – which other Andalusian cities did not benefit from at all – Málaga now has three Picasso centres: the Picasso museum in Palacio de los Duques de Buenavista, another Picasso museum in the restored bishop's palace and the house where Picasso was born, a regular site of pilgrimage for tourists.

In Andalusia, whose cultural scene is so far undeveloped, Málaga with its Picasso museums is a shining exception. In 2004 there were high hopes in Seville as Harald Szeemann hosted his ambitions 1st art biennale in a former convent on the La Cartuja, the island of the Expo, but, following the death of the renowned Swiss curator, the Guadalquivir city threatened to sink back into artistic mediocrity. And yet Seville has the Reales Atarazanas, a fantastic exhibition venue. This is a shipyard originally built at the instigation of Alfonso the Wise in the 13th century, an archaic-looking site with massive arcades and vaults. Back in 2004, the Andalusian artist Pilar Albarracín breathed unexpected new life into the Reales Atarazanas with her ironic take on Spanish myths. In fact, Seville has several potentially fascinating art venues that it should make more use of. Another of these is the Cuartel del Carmen. This medieval convent was used as a barracks during Franco's rule. It was abandoned at the end of the eighties and shortly afterwards became an exhibition centre for a short time. In 1988, the American artist Julian Schnabel installed his impressive show »Reconocimientos Pinturas«, here. Held anywhere other than in this remarkable building, it would not have been the same show.

Pioneering museum building projects are increasingly taking place on the Mediterranean coast – the region that profited most from the gargantuan real estate boom. Presently the most impressive projects are taking place in Valencia and Cartagena. Valencia's development is guided by urban planning – after the completion of Calatrava's Ciudad de las Artes y las Ciencias, reorganisation of the coastal zone based on the master plan by Jean Nouvel and Gerkan Marg & Partner is the next step – but the mood of the museum scene is also upbeat. Some years ago, the IVAM (Instituto Valenciano de Arte Moderno), which houses an important collection by the sculptor Julio González, requested the Japanese team Sanaa to design an extension. Their creation expands the museum's overall area by 10 000 sqm. Kazuo Sejima and Ryue Nishizawa have put a 30 m high perforated metallic shell over the old building, creating a transitional zone between interior and exterior, closed space and open space, urban space and the art sector. At the 9th Architecture Biennale in 2004 in Venice, this design received the Golden Lion, but for political and legal reasons the decision on planning permission has been indefinitely postponed.

Cartagena, another Andalusian city, is also investing in prestigious projects. In autumn 2008, Guillermo Vázquez Consuegra, who previously built the Museo Valenciano de la Ilustración y de la Modernidad (MUVIM) in Valencia, completed the Museo Nacional de Arqueología Marítima. The Seville-born architect divided the museum complex into two volumes: a transparent zigzag building to house the research programme and an opaque prism with a skylight for the exhibition space. As the museum is devoted to the underwater world, Vázquez Consuegra situated much of its content underground. Long-time leading figure Rafael Moneo has taken on an entirely different project in Cartagena. After the excavation of the Roman amphitheatre directly next to the church of Santa María la Vieja in recent years, the decision was made to design not only an archaeological garden but also an exhibition space for the excavated objects. Moneo's project is highly complex because it means intervening in the city's structure, with a museum concept that makes intelligent use of both old and new buildings. Rafael Moneo's Cartagena project complements other archaeological museums in Andalusia witnessing to southern Spain's rich Roman and Arabic heritage.

Alberto Campo Baeza's Museo de la Memoria de Andalucía in Granada – one of the projects presented at the New York MoMA exhibition »OnSite: New Architecture in Spain« at the beginning of 2006 – also stands out among the museum buildings that will be part of Andalusia's future cultural landscape. Campo Baeza proposes a clear structure for the museum complex, with a narrow slice taken up by administration and a sunken exhibition area at the front, reached via impressive spiralling ramps.

This ambitious project by the home of the Moorish Alhambra marks a change of policy for Andalusia's cultural centres whose repercussions can be felt most of all in Córdoba, former capital of the Caliphate of Córdoba. Here on the Guadalquivir, the Madrid architect Juan Navarro Baldeweg has created a landscaped park, opening Córdoba out onto the river once again. On the other bank – where the modern town is to stand – Rem Koolhaas is to build the Palacio de Congresos, with the Madrid architects Nieto and Sobejano's Espacio de Creación Artística Contemporánea (a centre for media art) directly next to it – a promising art centre based on the geometrical spatial structure and decorative patterns of the Córdoba mosque, creating a connection with the Moorish past. Fuensanta Nieto and Enrique Sobejano see the centre as a repeating spatial formation created by variations on three hexagonal

4. Alberto Campo Baeza, Museo de la Memoria de Andalucía, Granada, 2009. Building this museum is intended to reduce northern Spain's dominance in terms of cultural institutions.

ground plan outlines rather than a unified spatial organism. The regularly perforated façade is also intended to evoke the famous mosque.

Recently the southern regions have also been able to attract international stars. For instance, Zaha Hadid is building a university library in Seville and Herzog & de Meuron completed the Tenerife Espacio de Arte (TEA) in Santa Cruz de Tenerife at the end of 2008. In the culture centre there is an extensive collection of paintings by the locally born painter Óscar Domínguez (1906–1957), an aficionado of surrealist art circles in Paris. The exhibition space is dedicated to international contemporary art and aims to become an »international reference point«. The massive competition from similar art centres makes a glittering outer shell designed by an international star essential. It is, however, questionable whether Pritzker Prize winners can help to create an impressive museum repertoire as well as improving a city's image.

As the state in Spain has followed the trend in increasingly relinquishing its cultural responsibilities, many foundations, large and small, have sprung up to fill the gap thus created. Undoubtedly the most influential is the Catalan la Caixa, a subsidiary of the regional bank of the same name. The foundation works on a fairly simple system. It receives 37.6% of the profits from la Caixa in Spain. In 2008, this came to an impressive annual budget of 500 million euros available to the foundation, with 79 million euros available for cultural activities alone. In Barcelona – site of its head office – the la Caixa foundation exclusively finances two large museums: the science museum CosmoCaixa, one of the first cultural buildings built in the post-Franco era and the CaixaForum, one of Barcelona's most impressive monuments to Modernisme, which was perceptively turned into an art centre by Arata Isozaki in 2002. The leadership of la Caixa then decided to build a central art hall in the historical centre of Madrid, and commissioned the Basel architects Herzog & de Meuron. Aside from the powerful la Caixa in Catalonia, it is the smaller foundations that are the cultural scene's

major support, and not only in the big cities. The best-known example of this relatively new Spanish trend is the Fundación Eduardo Chillida – Pilar Belzunce, which is responsible for the unique sculpture park Chillida-Leku in Hernani, not far from San Sebastián. Another example is the Consorcio Museo Vostell Malpartida, which manages a Fluxus collection instituted in Malpartida de Cáceres by Wolf Vostell in the midst of a breeding area for white storks in the heart of barren Extremadura.

Another unusual project has existed for some time in the very south of Spain, directly on the Strait of Gibraltar. 30 km east of Cádiz, among pines, cork oaks and olive trees, a sculpture meadow was created on the site of a military facility once used to guard the natural frontier with Morocco. Works by the Irish Olafur Eliasson, the Serbian Marina Abramovic and the Spanish Santiago Sierra among others are now exhibited here in the open air. In addition to these, new artworks are continually being presented in small exhibition pavilions. The Chinese artist Huang Yong Ping, for instance, borrowed from Western bunker architecture for one of his two pavilions and from the Arabic hammam for the other. His highly symbolic work encapsulates the contradictions of our modern world in this geographically strategic point between the continents. The South African Berni Searle's video installation *Home and Away* powerfully addresses the issue of African migrants flooding into the Costa de Luz. The site where these were staged has the initially difficult name Centro de Arte Contemporáneo Montenmedio de Vejer de la Frontera. As this does not exactly trip off the tongue even if one is Spanish, it has acquired the unofficial acronym NMAC. The downside of the Andalusian foundation's artistic merits is their commercialisation. Its advertising is dominated by entertainments with nothing to do with art – golf, equestrian sport, even motocross racing. Anyone visiting the Costa de Luz art centre must accept it as part of a larger entertainment park.

The Spanish foundation with the longest history is linked with the names of possibly the most im-

5. Josep Lluís Sert, Fundació Joan Miró, Barcelona, 1975. It was the first modern museum in Spain.

portant Catalan artist and architect: Joan Mirò and Josep Lluís Sert. Its design dates back to 1968, when many architects in Barcelona hoped that Sert would bring back the glory days of the GATCPAC (Grup d'Arquitectes i Tècnics Catalans per al Progrés de l'Arquitectura Contemporània) during the Second Republic, when he collected architecture's avant-garde together and created several important buildings in his home town. In 1952, Oriol Bohigas, who was president of the Fundaciò Joan Mirò and chief planner for Barcelona in the eighties, wrote to Sert: »The battle against Spanish architecture's stupid banality in recent years is wearing us down. When you finally come to join us, we will be in better spirits and be inspired to new efforts.«[3] Sert, who was made a dean at the Graduate School of Design in Harvard in 1953, did not come to the metropolis on the Mediterranean until much later, after the opening of the museum and the death of Franco in 1975. He held no hopes for Barcelona while Franco's dictatorship existed, and so he designed the museum for the Miró foundation faraway in his studio in Cambridge. He chose the Montjuïc hill as the site, so that the building would be better screened from the cityscape. The museum was built in the last stages of Franco's regime and represented a relaxation of cultural politics. Architects like Oriol Bohigas, José Antonio Coderch, Óscar Tusquets, Ricardo Bofill and Manuel de Solà-Morales were able to continue and reinvent the avant-garde architecture of the thirties during this period.

Josep Lluís Sert based his museum building on his design for the Fondation Maeght in Saint-Paul-de-Vence in France (1964). He created skylights, a clear system of passages through the building, and gardens and terraces adapted to the layout of the museum's rooms and its situation. The museum ensemble consists of small units grouped around an inner courtyard. Sert used modern materials like concrete, but also incorpo-

rated regional building traditions like the Catalan vault and tiled floor. In the last twenty years, project director Jaume Freixa was twice commissioned to add extensions to the museum building suited to Sert's structural logic.

Three dates are of primary importance to Spanish modern architecture. In 1926, after the death, caused by a tram, of Antoni Gaudí, the popular modernisme, the Catalan variety of Art Nouveau, began to decline. Barely two years later, the architects of Barcelona joined the general enthusiasm for Le Corbusier. At the time, the Frenchman was the new star in the firmament of international architecture. Josep Lluís Sert invited him to lectures in the Catalan metropolis. Le Corbusier was unimpressed by Gaudí's buildings, but the provisional schools next to the Sagrada Familia cathedral (largely forgotten today) did interest him. He recorded the wavelike curves of their roof in his famous notebook. On the other hand, he paid no attention to La Pedrera and Sagrada Familia.

Another crucial date was the year 1929. On the occasion of the World Exhibition, Mies van der Rohe dressed up in the traditional top hat and tails to open his legendary pavilion on the Montjuïc, which, in a town that was still a bastion of traditional Noucentisme, looked like a building from another world. Mies' understanding of construction techniques and spatial arrangement gradually made an impact on the nascent Catalan avant-garde surrounding Sert. The year 1929 also saw an architectonic emergence in Seville in Andalusia, where the World Exhibition on the Guadalquivir was characterised by a revival of traditional historicism. It was no accident that Spanish architecture was gradually opening up at this particular time. At around the same time, the regime of Primo de Rivera stepped down and Spanish society began to become more democratic, culminating in the proclamation of the 2nd Republic in 1931. During this short but turbulent time – during which Barcelona and Madrid became avant-garde centres – architects like Erich Mendelsohn, Theo van Doesburg and Walter Gropius travelled to Spain to give lectures. The Catalan capital in particular became a cosmopolitan metropolis: J. J. P. Oud's Dutch housing developments were echoed in experimental minimum subsistence housing units and Le Corbusier's »Immeuble Villa« design gave rise to the collectively designed »Casa Bloc« (1932/33), an open residential block with maisonette apartments and communal facilities. Like the Dessau Bauhaus, the GATCPAC, founded by Sert in 1930, aimed to improve living conditions in society and to create social housing. Sert's collaboration with Catalonia's government was full of potential. Both were looking for a new direction after the Rivera dictatorship, and they chose International Style architecture and urban planning. The government commissioned the GATCPAC architects to design rational housing outside the Cerdà expansion area. The new collective goals also included urban planning projects, including developing the Avenida Diagonal, a public road running through Barcelona, which was to be designed on the principles of the legendary CIAM congress »The Functional City«. Of equal importance was the »Barcelona Futura«, the new overall plan for Barcelona negotiated by Sert and Le Corbusier with the Catalan president Macià in 1932, after whom it was named. This plan, which was never to be implemented, was developed in close collaboration with Le Corbusier and has a place in the history of modern urban planning.

The next important event did not take place until 1992. During the economic boom, the Olympic Games gave Barcelona its first opportunity to really explore the concepts of classical Modernism. Vittorio M. Lampugnani wrote that the aim had been to reconcile Le Corbusier, Pierre Jeanneret and Josep Sert's Plan Macià with Ildefonso Cerdà's »Eixample«.[4] To mark the Olympic Games, Oriol Bohigas the influential departmental head for planning had major urban projects carried out by numerous international architects like Norman Foster, Arata Isozaki and Vittorio Gregotti and succeeded remarkably in reviving the city's compact pattern. Bohigas also invited many artists including Richard Serra, Claes Oldenburg, Eduardo Chillida, Ulrich Rückriem, Ellsworth Kelly and Rebecca Horn to create sculptures for Barcelona's entire area. This initiative benefited the outskirts as well as the inner city – their public areas were expanded by the building of ramblas, squares and parks. Peter Buchanan saw this as »a total redesign of Barcelona«.[5] The old town was not left out. For instance, Garcés/Sòria expanded the Picasso museum in Barrio Gótico and Viaplana/Piñon transformed the Casa de la Caritat in neighbouring Raval into the Centre de Cultura Contempòranea de Barcelona (CCCB) and finally the New York architect Richard Meier built the Museu d'Art Contemporani de Barcelona (MACBA) – the highlight of the architectural, cultural and social renewal of the Ciutat Vella.

Oriol Bohigas commented that the short period of architectonic experimentation had ended abruptly in 1939, when the Franco regime became established. For this reason, it was important to Bohigas to reconnect with the achievements of the Spanish avant-garde of the twenties and thirties after the move towards democracy

in 1975. The revivalist trends since the fifties show that these achievements had never been entirely buried – witness the serial housing developments by Fernández del Amo in Vegaviana, Alejandro de la Sota's governmental building in Tarragona and Sáenz de Oiza's Torres Blancas in Madrid. Bohigas, who was director of the Escuela de Arquitectura de Barcelona from 1977 to 1980, believes that Spain was fortunate enough to be spared the interruptions to architectural development created in Germany by National Socialist architectural ideology. Instead, a »Spanish Rationalism« was allowed to develop at the fringes of the International Style, different from it in certain respects. Bohigas sees this as a style »distinguished by critical maturity and the will to go beyond initial idealistic concepts and design and architectural utopias by reclaiming regional traditions, by clearly understanding constructive systems and real social need and by a certain eclectic style«.[6]

Kurt W. Forster once said that Spanish architecture had experienced a phenomenal boom after Franco's death, turning Spain into an »architectural laboratory«.[7] At the beginning of 2006, when Terence Riley organised the MoMA exhibition »On Site. New Architecture in Spain«, the Madrid architecture historian Luis Fernández-Galiano brought out a special edition of the magazine *Arquitectura Viva* entitled »Spain Builds. Arquitectura en España. 1975–2005«. In this volume, the American critic Kenneth Frampton attributes the same continuous qualities to Spanish architecture as Oriol Bohigas does: »The primary characteristic of Spanish architecture is surely its relationship with topography. Its secondary characteristic is its tectonic properties, the ubiquitous poetry of the construction, which can be seen in very different types of building. This can lead to Spanish architecture appearing extremely laconic, or even decidedly anti-spectacular. (…) Spanish buildings generally have a tectonic component far removed from media-oriented consumerism and from reductionism of the ›decorated shed‹ type. This architecture may lead to manifold interpretations and contradictions, but at its cultural heart it opposes the trend towards globalisation that is increasingly reducing the architectonic form to a comfortable, aesthetic product.«[8]

Spanish museum architecture since the late seventies – i. e. since the democratic »transición« – can be understood better when seen against this complex history. We can see a historical »continuity« in this architecture that runs in a direct line from Rafael Moneo's early Museo Nacional de Arte Romano (1985) in Mérida to his enlargement of the Prado museum in Madrid (2008).

[1] Julio Llamazares, »Arte contemporáneo«, *El País*, 5 Oct. 2004.
[2] Herzog & de Meuron, *Espacio Goya. El Museo de Zaragoza* (Spanish/English), Basel 2006, p. 9.
[3] Quoted from Josep M. Rovira, *Sert: 1928–1979. Half a Century of Architecture. Complete Work*, Fundació Joan Miró, Barcelona 2005, p. 325.
[4] Vittorio Magnago Lampugnani, »De Sevilla a Barcelona«, in: Luis Fernández-Galiano, *Spain Builds. Arquitectura en España. 1975–2005* (Spanish/English), special edition of *Arquitectura Viva*, Madrid 2006, p.132.
[5] Peter Buchanan, »Un florecimiento cultural«, ibid., p. 112.
[6] Oriol Bohigas, »Rationalismus und internationale Avantgarde«, in: *Architektur im 20. Jahrhundert. Spanien*, Munich 2000, p. 83.
[7] Kurt W. Forster, »España es un laboratorio, cultural y politico«, *El País*, 7. 9. 2004.
[8] Kenneth Frampton, »Banderas al viento«; in: Luis Fernández-Galiano, loc. cit., p. 86.

Respectful extension

The re-opening of the Prado in October 2007 received widespread attention. Rafael Moneo's extension will further enhance the allure of the Prado and of the new Madrid museum ensemble as a whole. In this interview, Moneo talks about how his extension respects Villanueva's museum's architectonic style as far as possible, without totally avoiding modern styles.

Klaus Englert: Your extension to the Prado was completed this spring, after five years of construction. There was a legal battle lasting several years before it could be built, because residents lodged an appeal with the courts. What do you think about that today?

Rafael Moneo: The Prado is a very well-loved museum that everyone associates with Madrid. And so many people feared that any architectonic change would detract from the Prado's familiar image. My extension project, however, is very restrained, with a discreet structural logic and a precisely worked-out and well-considered space plan. Juan de Villanueva's Prado would be no place for an unconnected extension that violated the logic of all the earlier extensions. The extension therefore had to be built at the rear of the building. We built a tract connecting the two, whose role within the building is comparable to urban access infrastructure. My intervention barely changes Villanueva's Prado. The Museo del Prado always had a strong topographic element, and it profits from the recreation of the original difference in height. This was where my idea of how the old and new buildings should fit into the hillside behind the museum came from. This idea is a clear tribute to Villanueva. If he were still here, 200 years on, he might agree.

Klaus Englert: What do you think of the whole complex as it stands today?

Rafael Moneo: Once the Puerta de Velázquez opens on the Paseo del Prado and people can go directly from the old to the new building, they will be able to better understand Villanueva's architecture and its structure. In the past few years of the extension's completion, I was particularly concerned with the shape of the foyer's roof. Obviously I didn't want it to look like a supermarket. So I decided to lay out a classical garden on top. For me, this garden complex was one of the most interesting parts of the extension project.

Klaus Englert: How did you deal with the architectonic features of Villanueva's Museo del Prado and the historical extensions?

Rafael Moneo: There were two issues involved – the urban planning problem of improving the access areas in front of the new entrances, and the actual architectonic task of extending the exhibition space – although the two processes weren't mutually exclusive. My extension project aimed to understand Villanueva's palace, with its architectonic logic, and to expand on it using a moderately modern concept. I wasn't interested in building an extension that contradicted the Museo del Prado's essential logic. I think my annexe respects Villanueva's architecture without being spectacular in itself.

Klaus Englert: What made you use clinker – now used by very few architects – for the redesign of the cloister?

Rafael Moneo: I worked with this material when I built the Bankinter building and converted the Atocha station. In my home village, a lot of building was done in brick and ceramics, so I have a respect for them as materials. Some members of the Prado foundation would have preferred modern materials. But I think that a glass façade next to the Cloister of Jerónimo would have looked disruptive, and that using stone would have looked arrogant.

Klaus Englert: What do you think of Álvaro Siza's open-space plan? As you know, he wants to make the Paseo del Prado more attractive and connect the museums – the Thyssen-Bornemisza, the Reina Sofía, the CaixaForum and the Prado – together better.

Rafael Moneo: Siza takes his cue from Salón del Prado, the great project by Charles III. Personally I have always liked the lines of the Paseo de la Castellana and Paseo del Prado. They demonstrate the beauty and modesty of 18th and 19th century Madrid architecture. To some extent it was a case of making a virtue of a necessity. Because in Madrid they couldn't imitate the axiality of the Paris boulevards, they created the sequences and alternations of the Via Castellana.

Klaus Englert: Madrid hopes that the »Paseo del Arte« project will bring with it international prominence. Prado director Miguel Zugaza says that the aim is to emulate Berlin's Museuminsel. Is Berlin's homogenous ensemble like the »Paseo del Arte« in any way?

Rafael Moneo: As you know Miguel Zugaza wants to reconnect the remaining parts of the Palacio del Retiro. The envisaged »Campus del Museo del Prado« is certainly an ambitious project, but this new ensemble will not incorporate the other museums on the »Paseo del Arte«. There is no existing homogenous complex here, as there is on the Berlin Museumsinsel. It is more a case of architects seeking specific solutions that relate to specific sites.

Klaus Englert: The Prado extension is the most recent of several museum buildings designed by you. You previously built the Museo Nacional de Arte Romano in Mérida, the Audrey Jones Beck Building of the Museum of Fine Arts in Houston and the Moderna Museet in Stockholm. Which of these museums is your favourite?

Rafael Moneo: That's an easy question to answer. My favourite museum project was the first, the Museo Nacional de Arte Romano. The stylistic references to the Roman building style seemed particularly clear and appropriate, without any slavish imitation. At the moment I am working on a similar project which hasn't been publicized much thus far. It involves an archaeological museum being built on the site of the excavated Roman amphitheatre in Cartagena.

Klaus Englert: Spanish architecture – and particularly Spanish museum architecture – has been enjoying a resurgence since the 1980s. Why do you think this is?

Rafael Moneo: There is a huge difference between the Franco era and everything that came after the »transición«. During the France regime, there were hardly any museums and not much of a cultural scene. Since democracy came in in 1975, Spain has had a lot of catching up to do. Not only the major cities but also increasingly the smaller provincial towns of our 17 autonomous regions have invested in museums. The Museo Guggenheim probably showed many cities the way forward in more ways than one. Many communities followed its example, albeit with varying degrees of success. A few years ago, when I built the Fundación Beulas in Huesca, it was a question of building a small museum for the community – a place for art collections and for non-permanent exhibitions – together with a town park. But it varies from case to case. The MUSAC built

by Mansilla + Tuñon in León shows that there is a strong demand for cultural services, as do the museums they built in Zamora und Castellón.

Klaus Englert: Would you say that Spain has acquired a completely new attitude to culture within a generation?

Rafael Moneo: All in all, I think 1980 and 2007 were significantly different. Both cultural and architectonic interests are easier to pursue today than they previously were. This goes together with far-reaching social changes. Once upon a time, museums were elitist institutions that benefited only certain levels of society. In 1980, only the middle classes went to museums, whereas today it is generally recognised that museums have something to offer for everybody culturally. Today's situation would have been unthinkable a few years ago. Museums are speaking to people, and people are finding themselves attracted to the artworks. The visitors are actually proving themselves equal to the newly available cultural treasures.

Klaus Englert: Do the teams running museums see their role differently today?

Rafael Moneo: This may be one way the Bilbao Effect has changed the museum world's structure. Museum directors now play a larger part in cultural life and are better able to make their point of view felt. Think of the Centro de Arte Contemporáneo de Málaga (CAC Málaga). It has no international role, but it is very important to the city's cultural life.

Klaus Englert: What do you think about the many new museums of modern art that are springing up now, particularly in northern and central Spain? Is there enough material in the collections to justify this?

Rafael Moneo: Firstly, I think that both the north and the south do need new art centres, even though north and south have very different political and economic circumstances and networks. Regional government autonomy has achieved many things, with political and social transformation leading to a new cultural understanding – and a new role for art centres. A situation has been created in which museums raise the profile of the arts, and the arts influence the creation of the museums and their programmes. Of course this has also changed the role of contemporary Spanish architecture. A lot has been written about the boom in Spanish architecture since the 1990s, but this phenomenon should not be separated from the enormous accompanying changes in Spanish society. What the success and adaptability we see in Spanish architecture ultimately reveals is the dynamism of Spanish society.

Madrid, 10 May 2007

Victoria Acebo and Ángel Alonso, Centro de las Artes de A Coruña, A Coruña, 2007

In the winter of 2005/06, the Museum of Modern Art in New York organised an event to showcase recent Spanish architectural triumphs. A show entitled »On-Site« and curated by Terence Riley featured over fifty selected examples from all over Spain. Among these were two very different Galician projects. While the inclusion of the first of these – Peter Eisenman's »Ciudad de Cultura« designed for Santiago de Compostela – was hardly surprising, no-one had expected the Centro de las Artes de A Coruña by young Madrid architects Victoria Acebo and Ángel Alonso to make an appearance. And yet the newcomers had created one of the most innovative museum buildings of recent years.

Sadly, success in New York success was small compensation to the architects for the partisan conflicts that had dogged their museum project. In the summer of 2001, when Acebo and Alonso won the competition, the right-wing Partido Popular were in power at autonomous region, province and city level, and there were no problems in sight. The design by the two Madrid architects was chosen because of its original way of combining the required museum and dance school within a single building. However, the Partido Popular lost in elections during the construction phase, and the newly elected Socialist PSOE decided that as A Coruña already had a school of dance no facilities should be devoted to this purpose.

The plan for an institution with two different functions was abandoned – and this, sadly, was the death knell for Acebo and Alonso's excellent design, with its different functions developed around different transit networks. In the meantime, the Madrid Museo Nacional de Ciencia y Tecnología had declared an interest in moving its extensive collection to the new A Coruña art centre. If the Madrid institution has its way, there will be a fourth scientific museum in A Coruña alongside the Casa de las Ciencias, the Casa del Hombre and the Casa de los Peces. In the circumstances, it is questionable whether anyone will come up with a new plan to intelligently combine the two separately constructed thematic areas.

Disregarding these problems for a moment, the bay of A Coruña has gained a striking museum with the completion of the Centro de Arte. Isozaki's sail-shaped »Domus« rises at the end of the headland, while Acebo/Alonso's prominent glass cube stands out on the lower side of the bay, creating an additional landmark. Between the two buildings is a seafront promenade approximately 4 km in length.

The Centro de Arte de A Coruña is a surprisingly intelligent construction based around two separate thematic areas: the dance school and museum. The architects have written that: »our building is like two Siamese twins joined at the spine, unable to see each other but part of the same body – a single body formed of two different bodies«. This neatly describes the refined structure of the building, which, from the outside, looks like an unspectacular glass cube. Little, by little, a journey

through its inner corridor network reveals its structure, demonstrating the »duality« emphasised by Victoria Acebo and Angel Alonso.

Irregular concrete blocks project from a massive central concrete core. Each of these has a cavity and a glazed façade. These are the facilities for the dance school. The museum areas lie above and below these blocks at different heights. The architects used a double-shelled glass façade in shades of matted green with different cannelured effects rather than continuous glazing. Shot through with mouldings of different thicknesses, this glass façade also has a loadbearing function, as the thicker mouldings divert the tremendous loads created by the projecting concrete sections. Both thematic areas – the dance school and the museum – have their own entrances, which meet at one point only – where the midsections of the two »buildings« are connected by a bridge. The shared cafeteria, which offers an enchanting view of the A Coruña bay, is located here.

The five-storey Centro de Arte de A Coruña's split levels create an irregular storey arrangement which, in some places, creates extremely high lofts and, with a height of 28,5 m and a gross storey area of 5,057 sqm, the »Centro« is one of the biggest cultural institutions in Spain. We can only hope that a suitable new concept will be developed for the art centre in the future – a concept that fully does justice to its unusual construction.

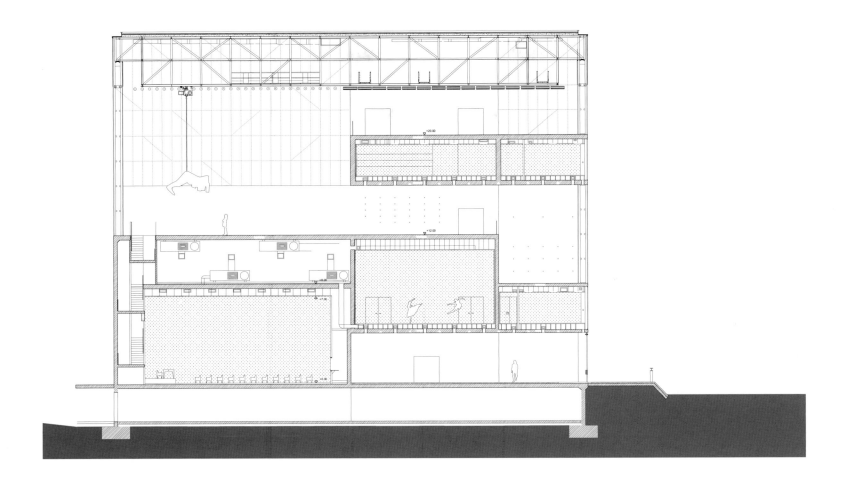

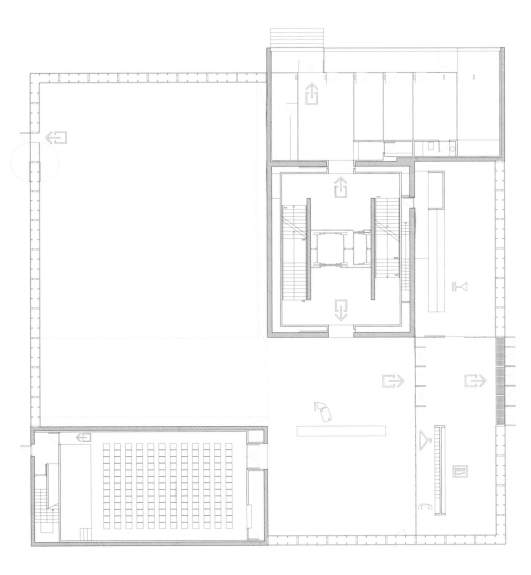

pp. 14, 15
1. View of the art centre, which is located directly on the Bay of A Coruñas.
2. Section.
3. Floor plan (ground floor) with entrance area and events hall.

4. Intersection of open und closed spaces. Dance school and museum.
5. Ensemble of concrete masses und open spaces.
6. Spaces as daring overhangs.

Manuel Gallego, Museo de Belas Artes, A Coruña, 1996

Manuel Gallego's Museo de Belas Artes in A Coruña occupies a special position in Spain's museum landscape. The Galician architect is known for reviving the peculiarly Spanish »paisajismo« style in the post-Franco era. This landscape-related style, as represented by early buildings by Coderch and Fernández del Amo, had been well-received since the beginning of modern architecture in Spain, but it was primarily Galician architects like Gallego (a student of Madrid university professor Alejandro de la Sota) who brought about this renaissance. Gallego's own residence is a manifesto for this architectural style (O Carballo, 1979), combining regional building materials with modern construction technology.

What stands out about Manuel Gallego's Museo de Belas Artes da Coruña is its sensitive approach to its urban environment. The museum building lies on the dividing line between the old Pescadería quarter and the open block structure of the less elegant new town. Gallego's museum project had to incorporate the ruins of a Capuchin monastery dating from 1715. Post-war urban development, speculation and increased urban density were threatening the sacred building's structure, leading to significant interventions in the fabric of the city. Documentary images from the early nineties show only parts of the monastery walls and isolated pillars standing. Gallego restored the building's main façade and wings and added a new building for museum use, creating a continuous structure enclosing the new museum spaces.

Manuel Gallego used a peristyle to surround the front courtyard, clearly separating the museum from the surrounding urban space. Gallego added the pillars to preserve the memory of the sacred

architecture that once stood on this spot. According to Gallego, they also represent a »grid« – one that opposes its own orderliness to its jumbled urban context.

The foyer's aluminium sandwich panels and glazing make it look surprisingly open and translucent. Gallego glazed the roof of the nave-like central tract and its rearward end, which offers a view of the old masonry. He based the foyer, which contains service facilities, on a pillar arcade, and distributed the exhibition rooms between the upper storey, the lower storey and a neatly added third storey, which is used for temporary exhibitions. Interestingly, the rooms that house the paintings from the collection have no view onto the street, as Gallego wished to avoid any contacts with the unsightly neighbouring developments. With the exception of the entrance area, all the museum's areas are therefore oriented inward. To compensate for this, Gallego created interesting internal views by cutting into different storeys, thereby turning them into open gallery tracts, and by creating lines of sight between the exhibition rooms and the atrium. Major design features include a wooden bridge across the freestanding central tract, which connects the three differently-designed museum tracts.

The Museo de Belas Artes da Coruña contains several treasures from the Baroque period, mainly artworks by José Ribera, Peter Paul Rubens and Annibale Carracci. Aside from 19th century Spanish landscape paintings, the collection is dominated by early modern Spanish artists inspired by *fin de siècle* Paris. Also of note are certain Flemish paintings from the 16th century. The beautiful Goya cabinet is like a treasure-trove, featuring engravings from *Disparates*, *Desastres de la Guerra*, *Tauromaquía* and *Caprichos*, as well as the Velázquez studies.

1. Site plan.
2–4. Floor plans (basement with service facilities and depot, ground floor with entrance hall and auditorium, first floor with exhibition halls).

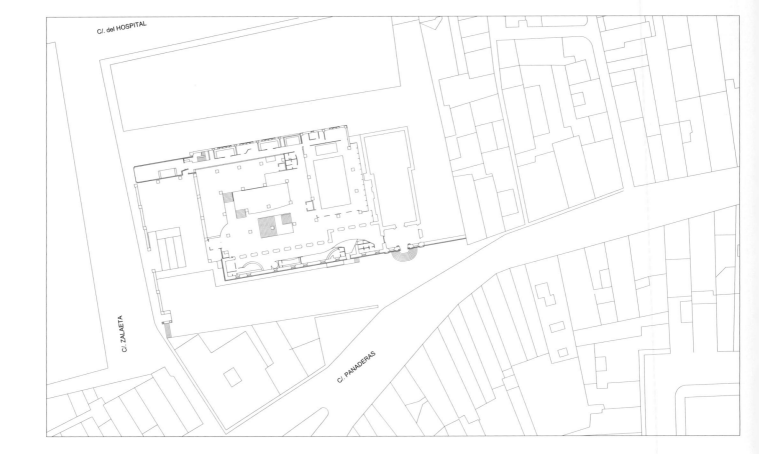

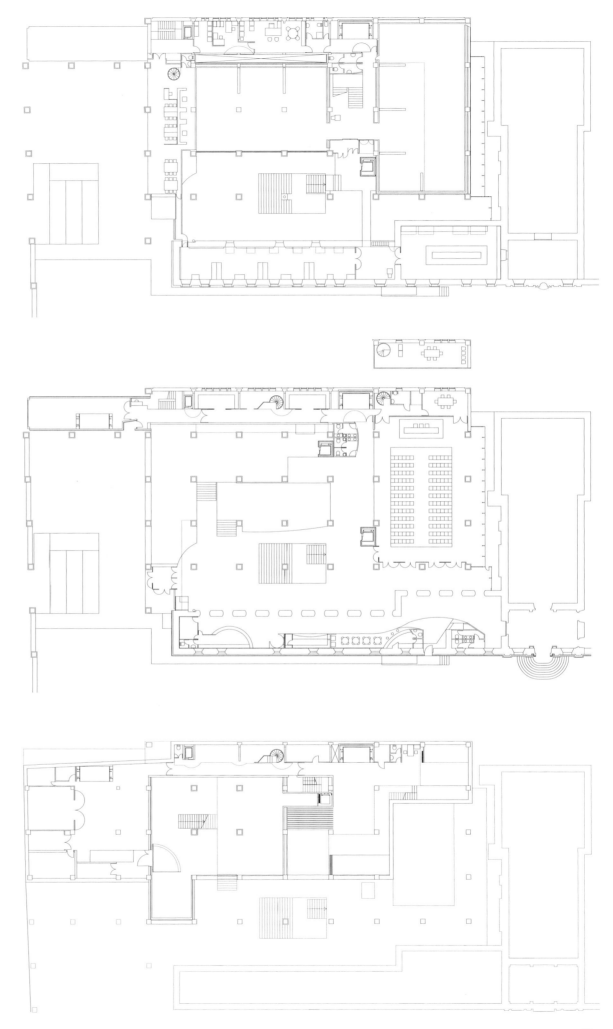

5. Area by the street façade, designed as a
peristyle.
6. Exhibition hall on the ground floor.
7. View through the atrium.

Nicholas Grimshaw, Fundación Caixa Galicia, A Coruña, 2006

Pablo Picasso, who followed his father to A Coruña in Galicia in his early youth, once called this north Atlantic coast town »the city of wind and rain«. The Mediterranean cities of Málaga and Barcelona made the deepest impression on Picasso; nevertheless, A Coruña must have had a very special charm for the young artist, who attended A Coruña's Escuela de Bellas Artes where his father taught drawing. Situated on a headland, the old town retains its charm today. Picasso would surely have been pleased to see the lively cultural location A Coruña has become over the past few years. The elongated west seafront promenade connects the glass cube Centro de las Artes building with the sculptural marine museum at the farthermost tip of the peninsula. A long row of buildings with traditional Galician glazed galleries stretches along the east side of the harbour, where the old and new cities meet. For a long time, a site within this long row and next to the Fundación Barrié de la Maza was the only construction gap in the fabric of the old city. Now it has been filled in with another foundation building; the Fundación Caixa Galicia, which has rapidly become the most popular cultural centre in A Coruña. Built by London architect Nicholas Grimshaw, it stands between the hubbub of the Pescadería quarter to its rear and the public gardens between the main road and the harbour. With its three narrow sections Grimshaw's cultural foundation is a novel and appropriate reinterpretation of A Coruña's glazed galleries – which nonetheless stands out clearly from the row of buildings. Like the traditional galleries, the glass façade erected by Grimshaw has maximum transparency – vital on this rainy Galician north coast. The glazed façade traces a parabolic course, first rising to the wavelike apex of the barrel roof, over the line of the building, and then falling to the ground storey behind, running downwards at an angle to the third basement storey. The sophisticated ventilating shaft installed by Grimshaw on the front of the façade provides even the two-storey auditorium beneath the foyer with sufficient natural light. A glazed, holographic projection wall suspended in front of the inwardly inclined façade balances out the extravagant façade design somewhat by echoing the vertical profile of the row of buildings.

The atrium is the connective element between the tower housing the access and gallery, the glazed elevator tract and the larger exhibition areas. The visitor's gaze rises through the air-filled space of the atrium to take in the building's ten storeys and its inner structure, moving along a sculptural stairwell carefully constructed from selected materials and the horizontal walkways that connect the individual exhibition areas. Varied use of marble showcases the construction's highly aesthetic materials. For the stairwell, Grimshaw used marble sections lit from behind; the marble comes from Namibia, and was processed in Carrara in Italy. For the façade, he used shutter slats made from fine glass and marble. These provide the interior with muted natural light during the day. At night, they turn the building into an illuminated tower that can be seen from a great distance.

Grimshaw's Caixa Galicia is a many-faceted building with not a few contradictions. It gives the impression of being a transparent, open and homogenous structure, but has clearly separated offices in the upper storeys and clearly demarcated exhibition areas – an internal arrangement that allows the Caixa Galicia to present several temporary exhibitions at once. Like the Catalonian Fundación la Caixa, the Galician savings bank foundation has its own collection and stages art exhibitions as well as organizing film festivals and book launches. Located at the entrance to the new city, the Fundación Barrié de la Maza and above all the neighbouring Fundación Caixa Galicia have succeeded, within a very short space of time, in considerably enriching the city's cultural life.

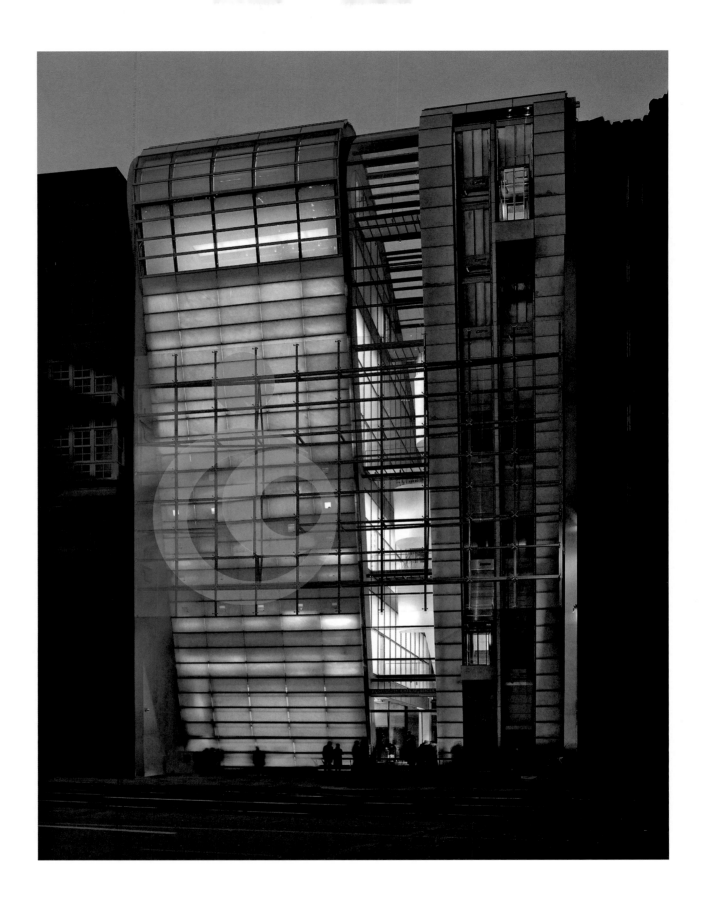

1. View from the harbour toward the Fundación Caixa Galicia (centre) and the Fundación Pedro Barrié de la Maza (to the left).
2. Night view of the Fundación Caixa Galicia.

pp. 24, 25
3. Basement of the cultural centre.
4, 5. Section with auditorium and floor plan (ground floor).

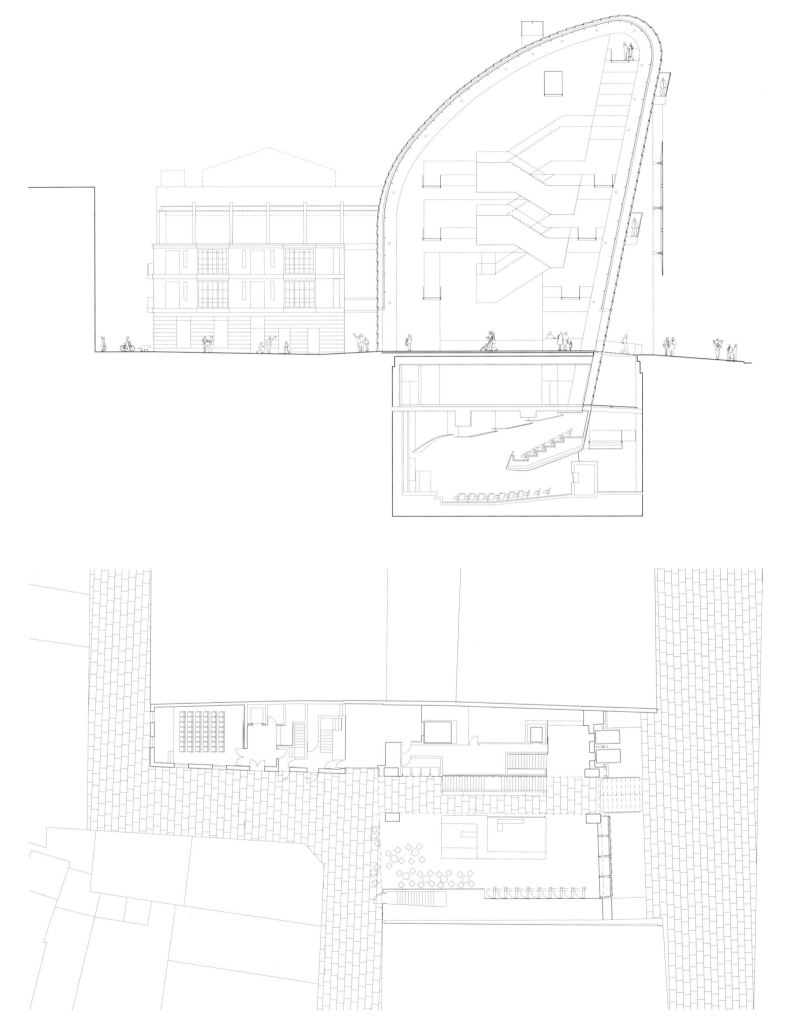

25

Arata Isozaki, Domus, la Casa del Hombre, A Coruña, 1995

At the beginning of the nineties, the city of A Coruña, which likes to call itself the »Balcony of the Atlantic«, wanted to build an interactive science museum of human behaviour to supplement the existing Casa de las Ciencias planetarium – and the Aquarium Finisterrae (or Casa de los Peces). It was to be called the »Domus« (or Casa del Hombre). A suitable site was finally located on the northern edge of the beautiful bay, which gives this Atlantic city a unique panoramic vista. Set on A Coruña's imposing headland, the »Domus« museum, which is 17 m high, has changed the silhouette of this section of the coast. Built on a granite outcrop above the marine promenade, Isozaki's museum looks like a huge, inflated sail, and is an impressive architectonic landmark, dominating the shoreline like a huge sculpture. Created by Arata Isozaki, the museum design was implemented by César Portela from Pontevedra.

The museum is reached from the shore via a ramp with steps that leads past a Japanese cast-iron warrior statue. The statue can be seen from a distance. Isozaki chose granite for the base, slate for the steps and terrace and concrete and slate tiles for the curved façade, which echoes the line of the shore. It was the emphasis on utilising materials from various parts of Galicia that ultimately secured the nomination for this architect.

The museum is an extremely simple construction. The basalt structure is demarcated by only two walls: the long parabolic concrete façade and a vertical rear wall made of granite slabs. The elongated, curved façade is made of prefabricated concrete components, with slate tiles as external cladding. The curvature gives the exhibition area a ground plan based on a circle segment and a cross-section based on an acute angle and a near right angle, meaning that it barely affects the exhibition spaces. In this respect, Isozaki's rear wall is reminiscent of a Japanese screen wall, with no significance to the construction, even though it consists of 20 cm thick granite slabs laid as cladding for reinforced concrete. On the topmost level, where the »sail« and »screen« walls come together, several pillars redirect the forces created by the façade's curve into the rear wall.

The interior of the »Domus« has a very open design, and the restaurant terrace offers a remarkable panoramic view of the seascape and cityscape. The exhibition levels are also designed like terraces, with ramps and stairs leading to them. All the floors are laid with slate tiles that beautifully match the materials used for the exterior.

On its ground storey, the »Domus« presents all kinds of technological inventions, which are greeted with joy by vocal classes of schoolchildren. In 2007, the remarkable temporary exhibition »Los otros arquitectos« was held in the rooms of the upper »Severo Ochoa« department. This exhibition told the story of architectonic development, and featured animal nests, organic cave structures, primitive mud huts and the architecture of today.

1. View from the seashore to the concave slate façade of the building.
2. View from the building towards A Coruña and the bay.
3. Jagged back front of the building with gardens.

4. The façade of the museum towering up from the rocks. In the foreground the terrace facing the bay.
5–7. Floor plans (lower floor, entrance floor with service facilities and terrace facing the bay, upper floor with exhibition area and auditorium).

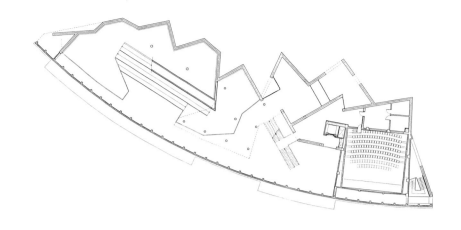

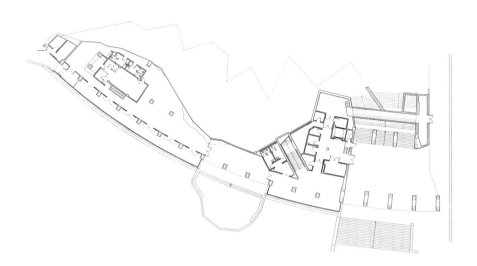

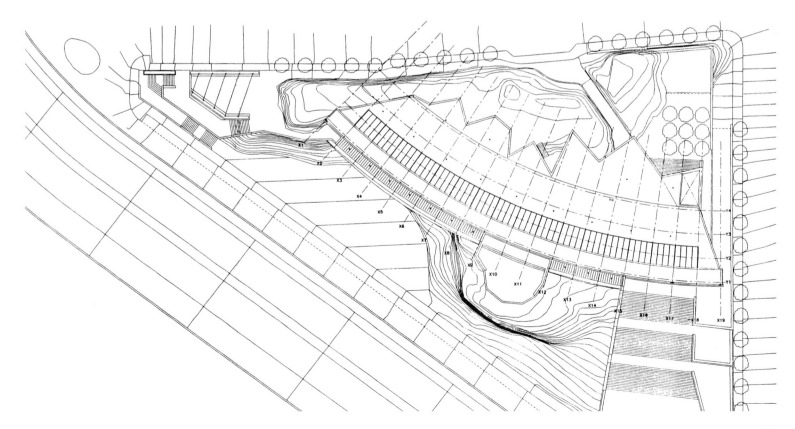

Alfredo Payá, Museo de la Universidad, Alicante, 1999

Along with sterile »experience architecture« and standard leisure facilities, the buildings constructed in Alicante previous to the year 2000 included a university campus with no equal in Europe for architectonic and landscaped beauty. It is hard to believe that not long ago army aircraft were taking off and landing on the site. The remaining former control tower witnesses to the complex's military past, but the campus feels more like an Island of the Blessed, where one can stroll over green lawns, beneath the shade of palm trees and past ponds, fountains, pergolas and sculpture gardens. The Spanish architects who built this campus proved that Spain's native architectural scene is of a high enough calibre to need no help from the »big names«. Álvaro Siza from Portugal – the sole non-Spanish architect – built a contemplative rector's office building in the form of a Spanish-Moorish hacienda. The University library by duo Pedro Palmero and Samuel Torres de Carvalho – a two-storey, elongated building with a striking »display window« feature – also makes a good impression, as does the architecture department by Dolores Alonso, a complex of three parallel L-shaped blocks.

The fact that Alfredo Payá, who had frequently collaborated with Alonso in Alicante, received only an honourable mention in the contest to design the school of architecture can only be considered a stroke of luck. Otherwise he would never have built the museum on the edge of the campus, which integrates so wonderfully into its bleak surroundings. Geometrical forms dominate not only

the exhibition buildings, but also the patio, the access ramp and not least the pond. All a visitor approaching from the direction of the university initially sees is the shallow square pool and an elongated, ochre-coloured block rising up in the background out of a depression. This is the body of the central exhibition pavilion, which is reflected in the water's surface. The partially roofed-over travertine walkway – a true *promenade architecturale* – which divides the pond provides an impressive entrance. It leads to a square located below water level. This introverted patio has the traditional southern Spanish openness, allowing the gaze to roam freely skyward or across the sparse local vegetation. It is a place of peace and meditation. The architecture creates an empty space in this »inner room«, deliberately avoiding any connection with the surroundings.

It is only when visitors have reached the sunken patio that they can see how the building consists of two sections running parallel to each other – the permanent exhibitions block, which can be seen from a distance, and a single-storey exhibition tract placed beneath the water level. Behind its storey-high strip windows, this tract provides rooms for temporary exhibitions. It is equipped with skylights that rise slightly from the water like steps. Payá added a lateral auditorium and amphitheatre in the open air to these two blocks.

The most eye-catching part of the ensemble is the central exhibition pavilion. It is surrounded by a suspended wooden volume made of compressed timber slabs with tropical wood veneer. The external façade seems to float atop the frameless, continuous glass wall. The loadbear-

ing beams were hoisted inside the hollow wall thus created. This is also a possible place for film or video presentations.

Alfredo Payá describes his design thus: »I see the university campus as a big garden. The pond is a part of this big garden, and the museum is a garden pavilion.« The major architectonic characteristic of the museum complex is its division into four areas, arranged in two pairs. On the one had there are the two exhibition areas, connected by a passage underneath the patio. On the other hand, there are the auditorium and the amphitheatre, which can be connected by pushing aside a glass wall. The impressive thing about the complex as a whole is its open perspectives and vistas, together with its minimalist conception and the way the two blocks relate to the landscaped water and stone around them. What we have here is a Japanese garden on the Costa Blanca.

The university museum's collection mainly consists of works by Valencian artists – including some by Eugenio Sempere, who met Eduardo Chillida, George Braque and Jean Arp during his French exile in the fifties and sixties. The collection also has 104 photographs by American architecture photographer Julius Shulman, who remained devoted to the »International Style« throughout his life.

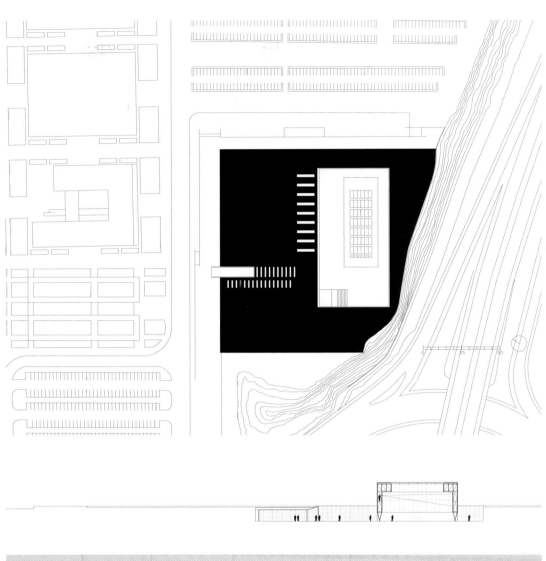

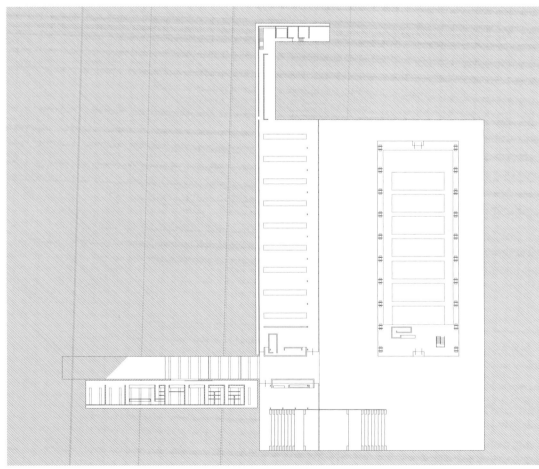

1. The museum in the middle of an artificial lake.
2. Site plan.
3, 4. Section and floor plan.

5. The entrance ramp to the patio and the museum.
6. Detailed view of the ramp.
7. The patio with the permanent exhibitions block to the right and the temporary exhibitions tract to the left.

Paredes Pedrosa Arquitectos, Museo Arqueológico, Almería, 2004

The province of Almería has many architectural treasures. The area was inhabited during the earliest period of human cultural development, as revealed by the Palaeolithic cave paintings in Vélez Blanco. The settlement of Fuente Alamo dates from the Bronze Age (2 000 years BC), and the Phoenicians arrived in the eighth century BC and set up the first trading posts on the coast – one at Cerro de Montecristo. The necropolis of Boliche suggests that the original Iberian inhabitants lived in settlements shared with the Carthaginians and Phoenicians, and the province of Almería also bears marks of the Roman colonisers who came later. Their rule here dates back to the third century BC. The Moorish Alcazaba fortress from the Taifa period (dating from 1 000 years AD) witnesses to Almería's less distant history.

The Archaeological Museum of Almería was founded in 1933. It had to close in 1994 due to the poor state of the building. Four years later and following a competition, the Madrid architects Angela García Paredes and Ignacio García Pedrosa were commissioned to build a new building in a contemporary style, and found themselves confronted with a densely built-up urban site with tall residential buildings and a circular road. They built a compact building to counteract these inhospitable surroundings. The building's front, which looks hermetically sealed, leaves space for a square with palm trees, giving this densely built-up residential area some public space. An already existing garden with palms on the long side of the building was extended to create a kind of attractive open air lobby in front of the exhibition areas. Although the building's façades have very different designs, the architects used the same material – marble from the Almería area – for all of them. Only in a few places does an opening in the compact façade allow a view of the museum's urban surroundings. Although the museum has a monumental look at first, the observer quickly sees how the gaps in the façade lighten its massive appearance.

Paredes Pedrosa Arquitectos designed a central airy space to help people find their way and connect the permanent exhibition rooms with the other display room sections. The staircase radiates expansive openness and creates surprising views reminiscent of Scharoun's Berliner Staatsbibliothek. The museum rooms are arranged into three levels adjoined by the wide access area, while the administrative rooms are stacked five storeys high. There are few windows in the outer walls; this allows full use of the rooms for display. Natural light enters this compact building mainly through the »sheds« on the roof facing northwest. To protect the archaeological finds as much as possible, these are fitted with light filters – diagonal strips of okumé wood laths, arranged so as to optimally absorb the intense sunlight.

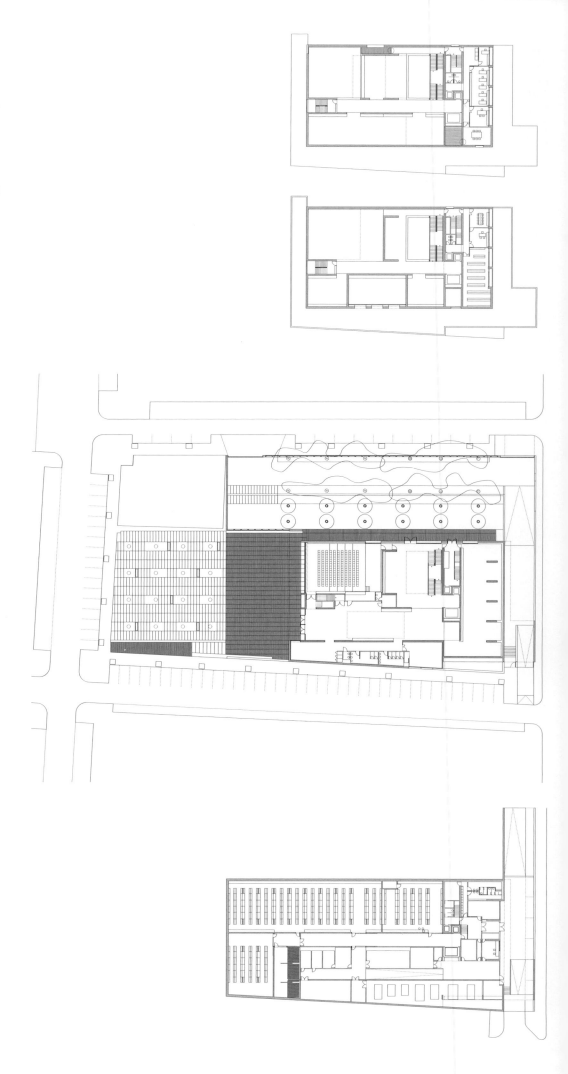

1–4. Floor plans (basement, ground floor with entrance area and auditorium, first floor with library and exhibition area, second floor with administration and exhibition area).
5, 6. The museum is secluded from its surrounding like a fortress with a hortus conclusus.
7. Section through the building.

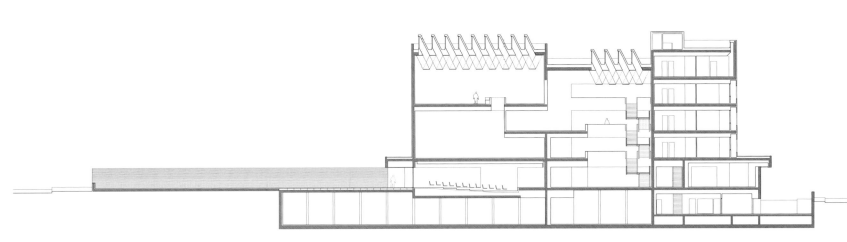

8, 9. The museum asserts itself against the busy street.
10. A prominent staircase connects the exhibition areas.

11. Diagonal strips of Okumé-wood slats filter
the natural light.
12. The particular organization of the floors pro-
duces an exciting space.

Javier Sáenz de Oiza, Museo Jorge Oteiza, Alzuza, 2003

The Oteiza Museum in Alzuza, a small community a few kilometres east of Pamplona, was built because of a decades-long friendship between the architect Francisco Javier Sáenz de Oiza and the Basque sculptor Jorge Oteiza. The two met at the end of the forties, when Spanish architects and artists created a kind of playground for formal experiments in sacred architecture. In 1949, Sáenz de Oiza won a competition to design the basilica Nuestra Señora de Aránzazu in the Basque province of Guipúzcoa. His building is composed of cubic elements and a tall campanile, with a façade decorated by Oteiza's famous frieze of the apostles. In 1954, Sáenz de Oiza and Oteiza were awarded the »Premio Nacional de Arquitectura« for their design for a pilgrim's church on the Way of Saint James, which sadly could not be built. The two friends also worked together on other competitions.

Together with Eduardo Chillida, a native of San Sebastián, Jorge Oteiza, who died in 2003, was one of Spain's most internationally renowned sculptors. In 1975, the year when democracy came to Spain, Oteiza and his wife Itziar Carreño finally settled in Alzuza, where he set up a workshop and a library for his aesthetic studies. A few years before his death, he asked Sáenz de Oiza to build a museum next to his house on the hill at Alzuza to house his artistic legacy. During Franco's era, Sáenz de Oiza, who built the organically-shaped Torres Blancas in Madrid (1969), was a

leading representative of a thirties-inspired architectonic avant-garde. Unfortunately, the Madrid architect did not live to see the Oteiza museum completed, dying in the summer of 2000.

Anyone approaching the Basque town of Alzuza from a distance will not get far before they see the museum, looking like a freeform sculpture perched on a slope. It takes a closer look, however, to reveal the purpose of the three strange craters on the roof: the prismatic skylights Sáenz de Oiza added to the reddish concrete cube. These skylights belong to an intimately lighted entrance area, while full-height glazed apertures and window strips provide abundant light to the exhibition rooms. The architect describes the guiding principle thus: »In a cathedral, the large windows light the nave, while only muted light reaches the side aisles. A higher degree of light energy corresponds to a higher degree of religious importance. The altar faces towards the incoming light of the setting sun. In the Oteiza museum, I wanted to create the opposite effect: a secular temple where the light comes in from the sides and the light that reaches the middle, where the rooms are dark and mysterious, is filtered. The building is like the faintly lighted and mysterious tunnel that Oteiza built in Aránzazu.«

Sáenz de Oiza wanted the connective tract, which conducts visitors to the basement and upper floor via black ramps, bridges and stairs, to look like Oteiza's tunnel. He designed the bright and variously shaped exhibition rooms, enclosed by pink exposed concrete slabs, to be a contrast to this connective tract. The contrast of light and

dark, pink and black runs through the whole museum. Sáenz de Oiza places importance on creating surprising visual contacts between the museum rooms and between the interior and exterior.

The fundamental architectonic concept was to unite the new building with the artist's home, which looks like an old-fashioned Basque country house. The museum's entrance leads into the house's former private rooms, which still have the atmosphere of a studio. The considerable library, attesting to the sculptor, poet and author's interest in the Basque language and culture, is also one of the central rooms of the Museo Oteiza.

The Museo Jorge Oteiza has a collection of about 2 000 works. The museum, which presents non-permanent exhibitions of the artist's abstract iron and steel sculptures as well as his drawings, is one of the most impressive museums built in the past few years, although sadly it is not well known. Alzuza is not the new, sophisticated Bilbao, and the restrained Museo Oteiza is not the glittering Guggenheim. Sáenz de Oiza also lacks the celebrity allure of the Californian jet set architect Frank O. Gehry. On a positive note, the Basque province is wonderfully quiet and tranquil.

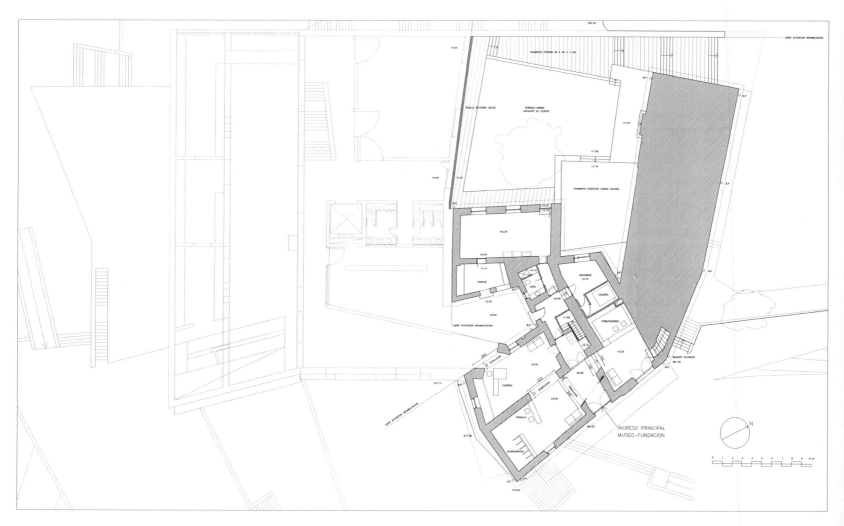

1. Floor plan of the museum and the artist's home.
2. General view with the city of Pamplona in the background.
3. The museum with the attached patio.

4–6. Exhibition rooms on the lower floor.

pp. 44, 45
7–9. Prismatic light wells dominate the upper floor.

Jordi Garcés and Enric Sòria, Esteve and Robert Terradas, CosmoCaixa, Barcelona, 1980/2004

The CosmoCaixa science museum shows that there is still a great deal of interest in this kind of museum in Spain. The comparable institutions in Valencia and A Coruña are in the same tradition. But the CosmoCaixa, built in the 1979/80 post-Franco period by Jordi Garcés and Enric Sòria is not just the oldest of its kind in Spain, it was the first important museum to be constructed after the dictator's death. Today this museum, which like the CaixaForum art galleries in Barcelona and Madrid is maintained by the la Caixa Catalan foundation, is one of the most interesting Spanish culture centres. It even won the »European Museum of the Year Award« in 2006, partly because of the lucidly articulated museum extension by Esteve and Robert Terradas, but also because of the extremely convincing museum concept. Cosmo-Caixa is in the westernmost part of Barcelona, on the Tibidabo hill formerly favoured by the local middle classes. Norman Foster's Collserola television tower can be made out in the immediate vicinity.

When Garcés and Sòria were commissioned in the late 1970s to convert Domènech i Estepà's 1910 home for the blind Amapaaro de Santa Lucía into a science museum, they had all the later extensions pulled down. They added a glazed foyer rising through the full height of art nouveau building and attached it flush with the façade of the old building. The architects chose a brick façade for the annexe, and its abstract two-dimensional quality provides an elegant contrast with the lavishly decorated masonry of the art nouveau building. The entrance hall, which affords a fine view of the neighbouring Santa María de Valldonzella nunnery, also dating from 1910, functions as an access area for all areas of the museum – the exhibition galleries and auditorium in the extension, the offices in the old building and the terrace at the back.

Architects Esteve and Robert Terradas added a considerable amount of extra space to these last sections in 2004. So the new CosmoCaixa now contains over 45000 sqm, and the gardens alone 6000 sqm. The Catalan architects hit on an unusual but simple way of extending the existing exhibition area by adding two more basement floors to the museum on its sloping site with two exhibition levels. Esteve and Robert Terradas decided on an escalator to provide access to the various floors, but also added a glazed cylinder docking with to the new basement storeys. A spiral ramp now runs round a gigantic »world tree«, connecting the individual floors via bridges. The cylinder and the exhibition building are supported by massive steel V-girders. The newly created public Plaza de las Ciencias with a café attached is a particular success. The copper dome of the planetarium thrusts out over the square like a gigantic sculpture. There is also a fine view of the nearby Tibidabo from here.

Perhaps the most unusual themed area in CosmoCaixa is the »Bosque inundado«. This is a replica of the Amazon rain forest with amphibians, fish, reptiles, insects, mammals, birds and numerous plants and trees. This rain forest recreated in a 1000 sqm greenhouse fully lives up to its name. It actually does start to rain every twenty minutes, to ensure constant humidity.

6. The Plaza de las Ciencias.
7. The Plaza de las Ciencias with view of the cupola of the planetarium.
8. The »world tree« spiral staircase.

3. The sunken entrance and the two steel trees in the background.
4, 5. The two steel trees with glass roof contrasting with the old building.

pp. 58, 59
5. The MACBA with its entrance ramp.
6. View of the MACBA and the documentation centre, which houses a library and space for temporary exhibitions.
7. View of the MACBA across the Plaça dels Àngels.

8. Public space on the ground floor.
9. The ramp leading from the ground floor to the exhibition space on the first floor.

10, 11. Exhibition halls on the second floor.

Frank O. Gehry, Guggenheim Bilbao Museoa, Bilbao, 1997

The legendary Bilbao effect is one of the most surprising phenomena seen in the international museum scene of recent years. It started with the Basque authorities' decision to revitalise Bilbao, a run-down industrial town on the banks of the river Nervión. New York's wealthy Guggenheim Foundation was brought on board, benefiting the Basques through its collection and international contacts. The Californian Frank O. Gehry won a restricted-entry competition organised by the New York foundation, beating Coop Himmelb(l)au and Arata Isozaki. Out of all the possible sites at his disposal, Frank O. Gehry chose the most difficult; a site in the heart of the Nervión's valley, next to a massive iron bridge and with a view of the opposing hillside: an unsettled site, from which Gehry's design gets its power. The rough, industrial charm of the town, the sheds along the harbour, the estuary dynamic, the hillsides – all of this is concentrated in his expressive architectonic sculpture, which has brought a phenomenal upturn to Bilbao in the past few years.

The artistic nature of this large-scale sculpture, which takes up 32 500 sqm, is accentuated by Jeff Koon's floral sculpture of a dog in the entrance area that faces the city and by Louise Bourgeois' oversized spider *Maman* on the river promenade. Clearly the museum's team have recently been trying to combat the belief that Gehry's titanium colossus is the only artwork of any significance for miles around, as they have sponsored numerous sculptures for public spaces. Koon's colourful and kitsch work *Tulips* was also purchased for the museum terrace for the ridiculous sum of 3.7 million euros. To mark the Guggenheim Bilbao' tenth anniversary in October 2007, Daniel Buren was commissioned

to create an artistic design for the neighbouring Puente de la Salve. The French artist decided to turn the bridge pylon into a »red sculpture«, a visual counterpoint to Gehry's gleaming titanium sculpture. He also applied his well-known black-and-white stripe to the sides of the bridge.

Although a building that looks like a mountain massif on the Nervión has had a lasting impact on Bilbao's cityscape, the building complex is not nearly as heterogeneous as it tends to appear in photographs. Gehry designed the administration building, which flanks the museum square facing the city, as a sober building with a sandstone façade and conventional windows. For the rear part of the museum, however, he abandoned any adaptation to the urban context, and created a tension-filled architecture.

The non-uniform construction of the different volumes reinforces this impression. Alongside orthogonal buildings with limestone cladding, one finds curved buildings covered with a metallic titanium skin. This titanium skin lends an overall impression to the whole building complex, even though the metal tiles are only half a millimetre thick. To light the museum areas, Gehry gave these stone and metal volumes dynamically hung curtain façades. The glass surfaces were processed specially to allow only filtered light into the rooms, thereby protecting the artworks.

Approached via the rearward promenade between the riverbank and the adjoining artificial pond, the Guggenheim becomes a dramatic architectural backdrop. A peculiar detail adds interest to the design for this part of the façade – a huge round tower topped with a baldachin and steel slat roof. The mighty glass façade thrusts forward behind it.

The main entrance is on the museum square, towards the city. A wide, dramatic staircase takes visitors to an expansive foyer. All the energies of

the building are concentrated in this foyer; this is the place where Gehry presents his construction principle openly. A kind of shaped box skylight, a »metallic flower« shines radiantly on the ceiling, providing light to the whole space. The slanting walls are supported by round concrete columns with bases clad in brown stone slabs and by a massive elliptical concrete support. Eye-catching bridges criss-cross the glass façades dramatically as they carry visitors on their voyage of discovery through the building. They make a perfect *promenade architecturale*, letting people penetrate deep into the museum's atmospheric world, allowing them to view the wide atrium and presenting views of the cityscape and the Nervión.

The expansive atrium gives the impression that in showing off his architecture Gehry is forgetting the purpose of a museum. However, the building also has 11 000 sqm of exhibition space – ten rooms with a conventional rectangular ground plan and a neat, compact stone façade on the exterior, and an additional nine gallery halls with irregular outlines, with a façade made up of curved shapes and titanium cladding. The largest hall is 30 m wide and 130 m long and for some time was used for special exhibitions. Since 2005, it has housed Richard Serra's *The Matter of Time*, a very impressive eight-piece series of geometric sculptures in Cor-Ten steel.

The Guggenheim Bilbao has staged many significant exhibitions in the past, displaying works by Andy Warhol, Eduardo Chillida and Anselm Kiefer. On the other hand, it takes its marketing strategy from Thomas Krens' New York Guggenheim Foundation, which in recent years has also staged some more questionable exhibitions dedicated to Armani or to motorbikes. It has been criticised for this by, among others, the Spanish author Antonio Muñoz Molina, long-time director of the New York Cervantes Institute. When the Guggenheim Bilbao

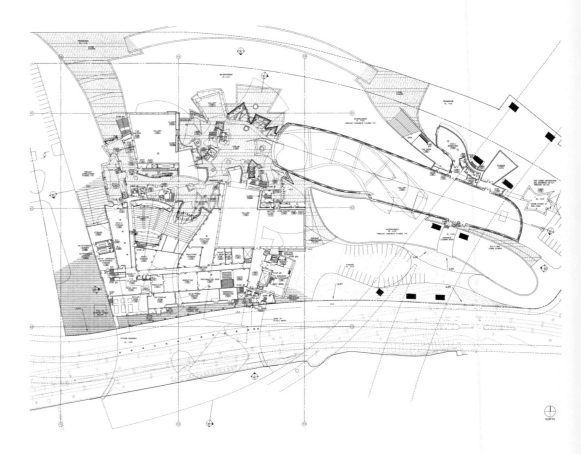

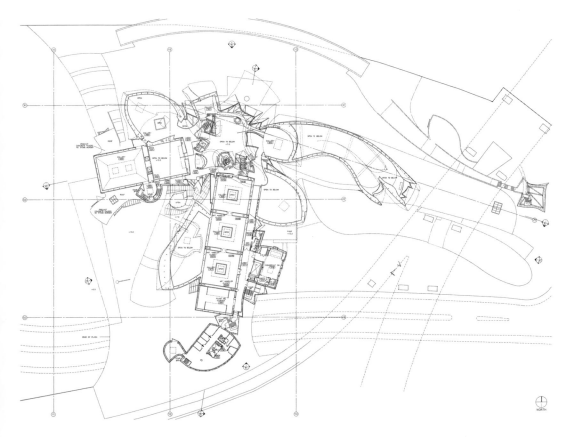

hosted »Russia« in 2006, a show from New York backed financially by the Putin empire, Muñoz Molina wrote in the daily newspaper *El País* that: »The Guggenheim has always gone for gigantism, for an overpowering orgy of images, for shocking exhibitions that spawn polemics among the established guardians of art. All to get the attention of the press, the public and collectors and thereby gain an advantage against other museums. The Guggenheim's role model is ›Wall Mart‹ – with its continual flood of new branches and staggering range of products. It has set out to co-opt entire countries – with the advantage that these countries will then provide lavish public funds to boost their own image, and their dignitaries will turn up at the vernissages together with their entourages.«

Since then, the Guggenheim Bilbao has increasingly come in for criticism. Its business management was accused of losing seven million euros through an arbitrary purchasing policy based on high-risk international exchange deals. Eventually the director of finances was accused of misappropriating 500000 euros. This seriously damaged the reputation of this flagship museum, which was for so long universally lauded as the birthplace of the »Bilbao effect« and which still managed to attract a million visitors in 2008.

1–3. Floor plans (ground floor, first floor, second floor).

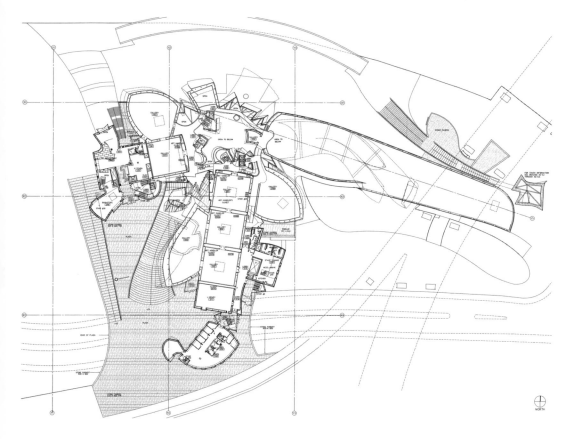

4. Evening mood at the Río Nervión.
5. A »baldachin« under the glistening firmament.

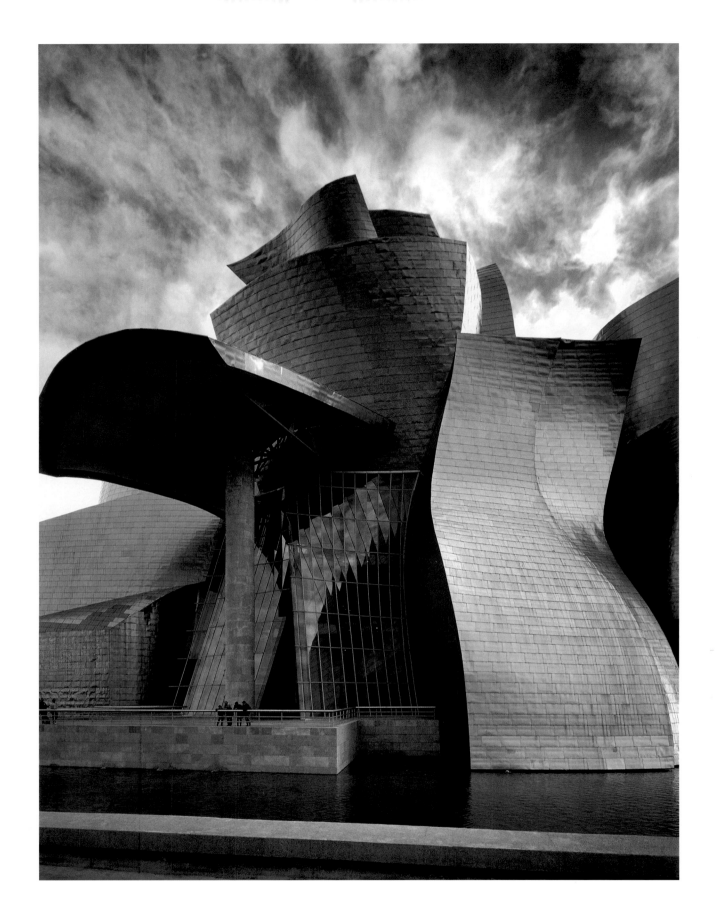

6. Feather decoration in the foyer.
7. Bridges, dramatically skirting the glass façade.

8, 9. The east gallery with a sculpture by Richard
Serra and a wall painting by Lawrence Weiner.

Rafael Moneo, Museo Teatro Romano, Cartagena, 2008

In November 1936, 32 planes of the notorious Legion Condor launched a devastating attack on Cartagena, killing over 1 300 people. They also bombed the medieval cathedral of Santa María la Vieja, leaving it in ruins. Because the Francoists saw Cartagena as the last stronghold of Republican resistance, Franco's air force, armed by Germany, launched a further attack on the enemy bases there in 1939, shortly before the civil war ended. This was when what was left of the cathedral's vault fell.

For a long time, the ruins of the cathedral were left to themselves, as a rebuilding project was never seriously considered. The story of the cathedral took a new turn in 1988, when Roman artefacts were found in the run-down district surrounding the ruins. The archaeological finds appear to date from the Carthago Nova period, when the Romans built their own splendid Carthago in the idyllic bay on the Mare Nostrum. To their surprise, archaeologists realised that the cathedral had been built over the upper part of a Roman theatre. Shortly afterwards, digging on a neighbouring site revealed that the foundations of the nearby bullfighting arena had been built exactly over the amphitheatre's walls.

Excavation of the theatre proved difficult, as dilapidation had set in long before. Even in late antiquity, market stands were being set up on the stage, and the structure's condition worsened dramatically after fisherpeople moved onto the site. The Arabic settlers who came later built houses on the terraces where spectators had

been seated. Twenty years ago, the Roman arena was invisible, hidden beneath the many dwellings erected in the barrio.

When archaeologists reached the bottommost layer, a relatively well-preserved semi-circular theatre structure was revealed. During the reign of the Emperor Augustus, it would have accommodated up to 6 000 people. The theatre is comparable to the Roman theatre in Emerita Augusta – today's Mérida – which has an almost entirely intact two-storey stage structure. The stage in Cartagena is almost totally destroyed, but this is more than made up for by the view of Cartagena's unique bay from the arena.

The renewed prominence of Cartagena's Roman past in its urban plan is largely thanks to Madrid architect Rafael Moneo who, 17 years after the first excavations, has turned the theatre into a real civic treasure. When he was commissioned to restore the imposing structure and to add an archaeological museum, he was working on the extension for the Museo del Prado. While he was creating a subterranean connection between the classical Prado, the museum annexe and the ruins of the Los Jerónimos convent cloister, he developed a similar solution for the ruins in Cartagena that allowed him to connect the different layers of the city.

The result was a complex urban project on three levels, incorporating a classical nobleman's palace, the medieval cathedral and a new small four-storey museum building and using two tunnels to connect them, with the Roman theatre as the grand finale of the journey. Moneo's design seems audacious, but in fact it makes a great deal of sense. Not content with merely restoring

the Roman monument and adding an exhibition space, the renowned Madrid architect's aim was a thorough-going urban revitalisation, complete with a park to round off the whole ensemble.

Moneo concealed the entrance to the museum complex, which is near the harbour, in the recreated Palacio Riquelme, so as to disrupt the façade opposite Cartagena's grand town hall as little as possible. This building's exhibition areas, and the continuous tunnel that connects with the new museum underground, are dedicated to the history of the Roman theatre in Cartagena and the excavations. The skylight-lit exhibition levels of the clinker-faced museum conclude by presenting the archaeological treasures brought out of the earth over the course of ten years, including almost perfectly preserved Augustus and Apollo statues, a gracefully curved semi-nude sculpture of the Vestal Virgin Rhea Silvia and the Capitoline deities Jupiter, Juno und Minerva, who were venerated in front of the theatre's stage.

Finally, a tunnel with thin brick facing that begins on the museum's top storey takes visitors through the 2 000-year long history of the location – leading past the calligraphic mosaic of a Roman house to the crypt and foundations of the cathedral, and ending with the impressive semi-circle of the theatre. This *promenade architecturale* through this area of high ground and through the layers of Cartagena's past shows just how unique Rafael Moneo's sense of urban space is among modern architects.

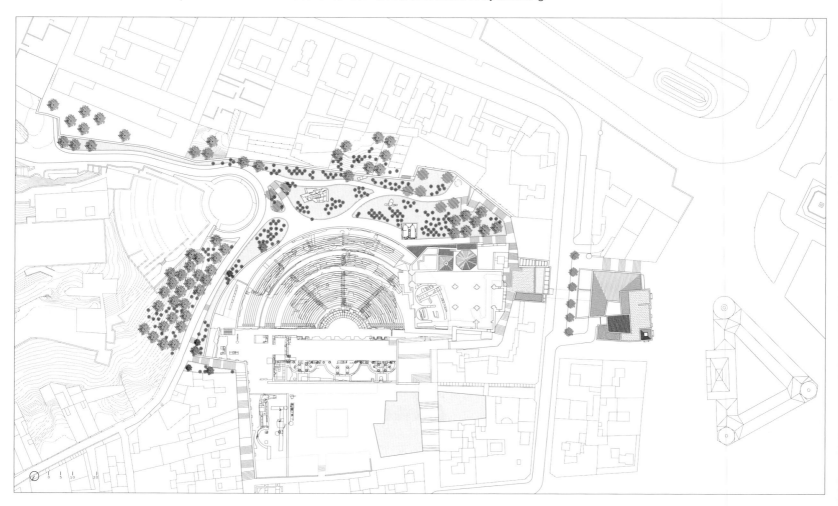

1. Site plan.
2. View over the Roman theatre towards the Bay of Cartagena.
3. The entrance area of the restored Palacio Riquelme.

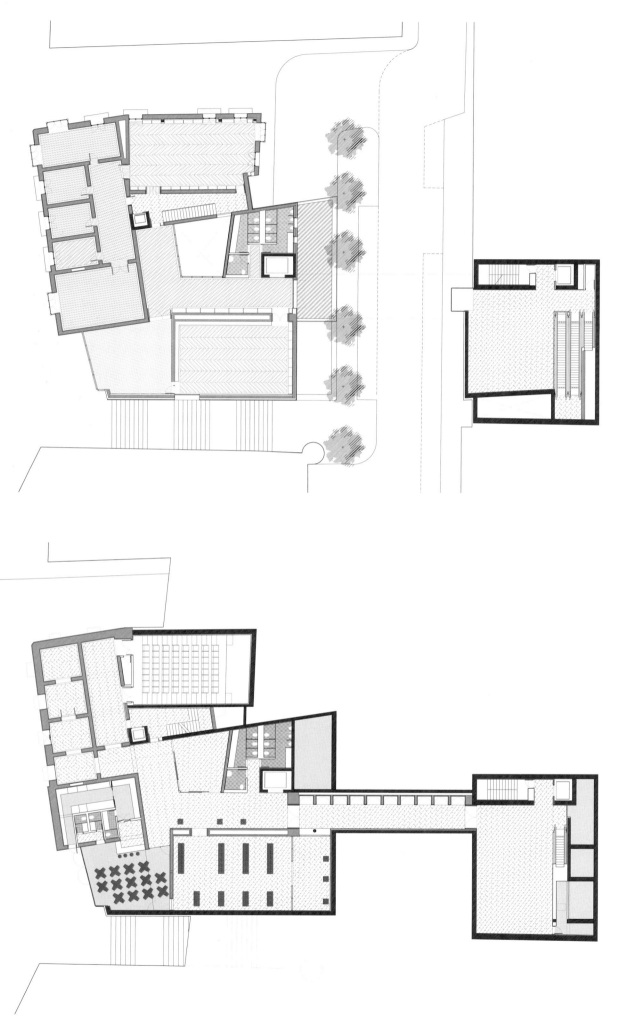

4, 5. Floor plans of the Palacio Riquelme and the new museum building with a subterranean tunnel connecting both.
6. Frontage of the new museum building.
7. View of an exhibition hall in the new museum building.

Guillermo Vázquez Consuegra, Museo Nacional de Arqueología Subaquática, (ARQUA), Cartagena, 2008

Some years ago, the municipal government of Cartagena decided to follow the example of Barcelona and Vigo by dismantling its harbour, thereby opening the city up to the sea. Since then, Cartagena has benefited from a new seafront, featuring restaurants, museums and a congress centre along a promenade with a road and an ancient Roman city wall on its west side. This new district has revitalised an old quarter dotted with Roman remains.

The marine archaeology museum designed by architect Guillermo Vázquez Consuegra from Seville opened shortly after Rafael Moneo's Roman theatre museum was completed. It fits brilliantly into the transformed harbour site. Unlike Moneo's neighbouring Teatro Romano, however, it deals exclusively with artefacts from the depths of the Mediterranean.

Thankfully, Vázquez Consuegra avoided the clichés of ship imagery, instead giving his research centre and museum ensemble a shape based on the topography of the site. The elongated research centre block, for instance, echoes the Roman city wall and the parallel line of the road, while the museum construction is an intelligent response to the nearby water. Anyone walking past

the exhibition building will be surprised by the zigzag ground plan and the inclined façade, but still more by the marine archaeology museum's whole extrovert nature, which allows passers-by to look into the lower exhibition level and see some of the objects brought up from the sea floor, putting them in the position of divers getting their first sight of undiscovered treasures from a distance. In this way, the broad glazed front creates a direct contact between the interior and the exterior, while the research centre block gives a slightly more aloof impression.

This ensemble's two parts look heterogeneous at first sight, but they are connected by a shared access ramp. Set against the research centre's concrete façade, the small public space created by the zigzag lines of the museum creates a friendly atmosphere and integrates well with the palm tree-lined waterfront promenade.

The marine archaeology museum is quite unlike Rafael Moneo's Roman museum in that its presentation methods are geared to educational purposes, making it a popular choice for school outings. Its wealth of exhibits certainly has great potential. The museum's main attraction, which can be seen from outside, is a Phoenician ship that was excavated on the shore of the island of Mazarrón near Cartagena in 1993. The permanent exhibition also includes numerous Phoenician and Roman cult objects, amphorae, tools and coins.

1, 2. Passage between the two building parts of the museum.
3. Perspective sections through the ensemble.

pp. 80, 81
4–6. Floor plans (basement, ground floor, first floor).
7. Entrance to the space for temporary exhibitions.
8. The permanent exhibition in the subterranean area.

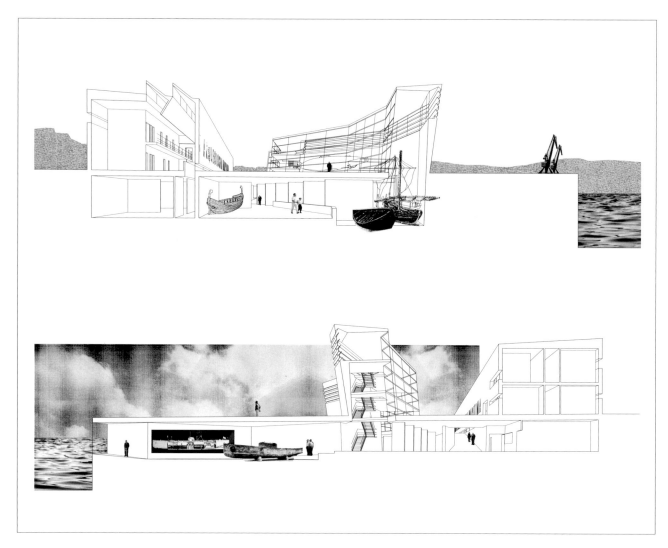

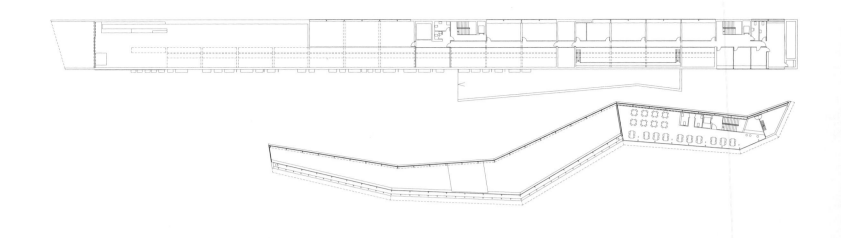

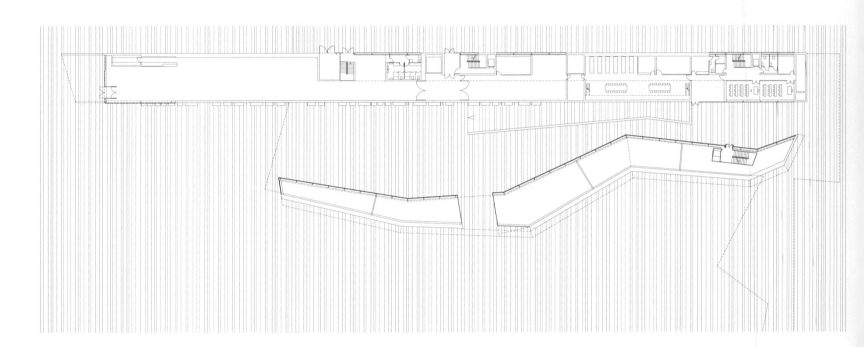

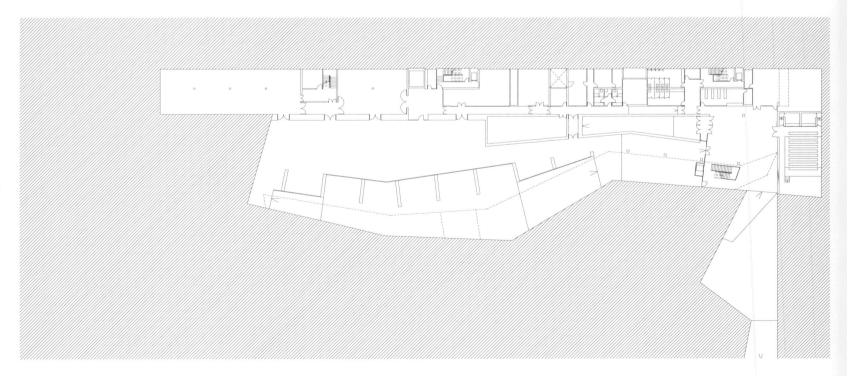

Mansilla+Tuñon, Museo de Bellas Artes, Castellón, 2000

The Museu de Belles Arts was the second museum building by the fledgling Madrid art duo Mansilla+Tuñon. They had previously built the provincial museum for the Castilian city of Zamora (1996). They later became internationally famous for building the Museum of Contemporary Art (MUSAC) in León (2004). In 1999, they won the competition to build the Museum of Royal Collections in Madrid. The art centre in Castellón in Valencia demonstrates the style of Luis Mansilla and Emilio Tuñon's work at this early stage. Their museum designs vary greatly, but there are formal similarities: the dramatic sequences of rooms and their varied treatment within a fixed system.

The Castellón museum rises from an oasis of cypresses, jacaranda and palm trees in the midst of a grey urban district. The neighbouring convent and the remains of the Serra Espadá foundation school complete this garden of the Muses. The exhibition area, arranged around the ecclesiastical complex, unites four different museums beneath a single roof – the ceramics museum, ethnology museum, archaeological museum and museum of fine arts. The five-storey building with box-shaped skylight extensions and a shimmering aluminium skin has a massive, fortress-like appearance.

The Madrid architects used a sophisticated »theme and variation«-based system for the interior, making similarly structured and fitted-out rooms give a totally different architectonic impression. This was the central idea behind Mansilla+ Tuñon's repeating, two-storey series of rooms fitted together around an atrium. This left laterally staggered gaps reaching down to the basement – a neat sequence of two-storey and single-storey elements. The dynamic spaces that dominate the provincial museum in Zamora are intensified to a cascade here, so that strolling through the museum feels like being carried along by a cascade of water. This play of room sequences, which gives the museum's interior a surprising lightness, is reflected by the seven colours repeated in different combinations throughout the interior. Both enthusiastic chess players, Mansilla+Tuñon have a vision of »theme and variation«, with a regular system containing many possibilities and variations.

The Museu de Belles Arts collection mainly includes church collections from the 14th to 20th centuries. Some of the exhibited works were taken from storage at the Museo del Prado.

1–3. Exterior views of the museum.

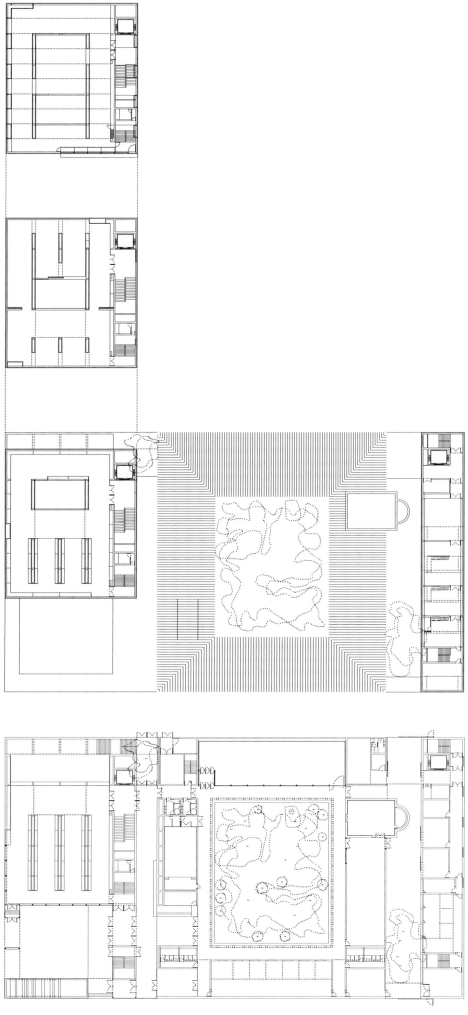

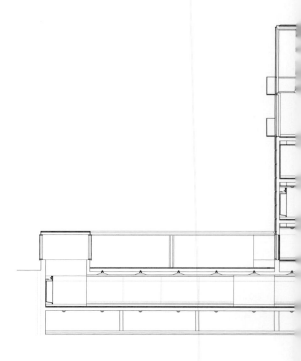

4–7. Floor plans (ground floor, first floor, second floor, third floor).
8. Section.
9. Exploded axonometric view of the complex showing also the interplay of the old and the new parts.

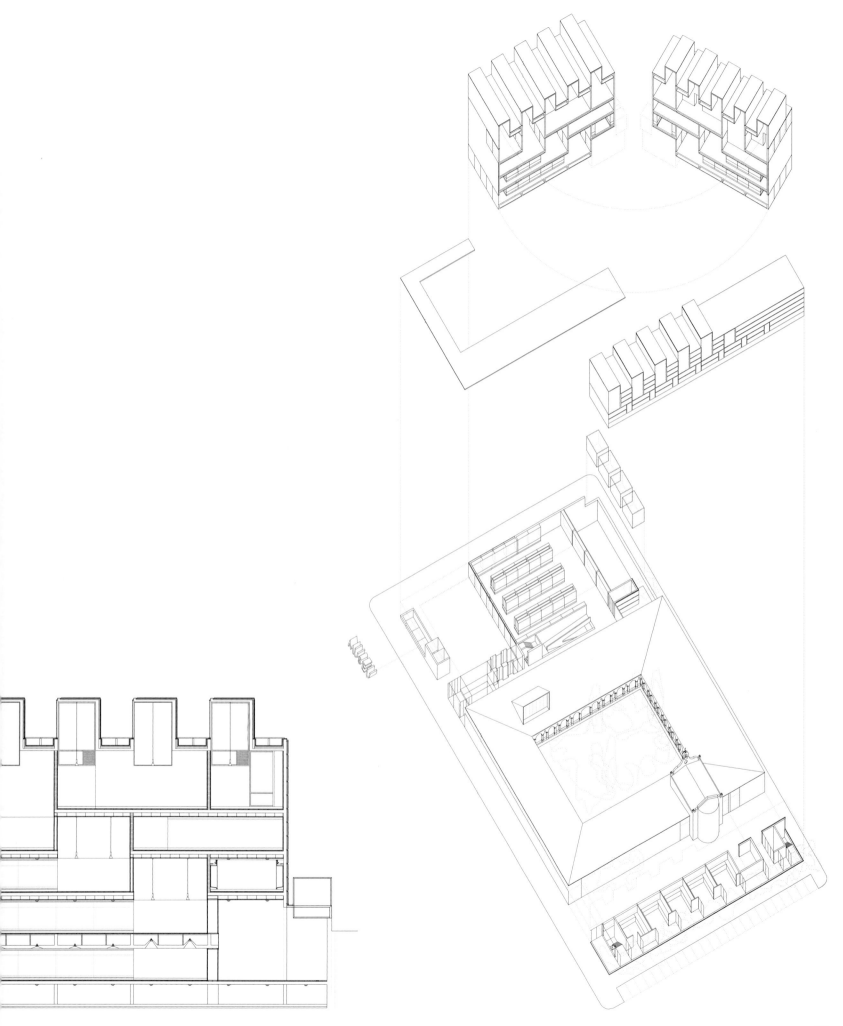

10, 11. The exhibition halls.

pp. 88, 89
1. The archaeological excavation site.
2. Site plan.
3. Floor plan of the museum with studios, offices and permanent exhibition.

4. Garden landscape enclosing the museum.
5. View over the roof scape of the museum.
6. The large patio.

Chillida-Leku, Hernani, 2000

Chillida-Leku is a sculpture park, the only one of its kind in Spain. The Basque sculptor Eduardo Chillida (San Sebastián, 1924–2002) completed it shortly before his death. The park is located on high ground 10 km from San Sebastián, with a view of the Bay of Biscay far below. In 1951, when Chillida returned to his Basque homeland after three years spent in Paris, he decided to work in iron, which meant learning the necessary skills in a smithy in Hernani. After much time spent abroad, some of it at American universities, Chillida returned to Hernani in 1984 and purchased twelve hectares of land together with a 1543 farmhouse. The farmstead, one of the oldest in the Basque country, needed extensive renovation, but for already world-renowned sculptor, it was a dream come true: »I had a dream of a utopia. I wanted to find a space where my sculptures could be at rest, and people could walk among them like the trees in a wood.«

Chillida-Leku's official opening in 2002 was preceded by year-round work by Eduardo Chillida, who had spent three years studying architecture in Madrid, and architect Joaquín Montero to restore the property. According to Montero, time and money were no object to Chillida's desire to transform the old »caserío« into an exhibition building. The sculptor himself talked about a »dia

logue« with the building: »I asked the building how it wanted to look. I walked through the rooms and investigated whether this wall, this partition or that mezzanine should be retained, and finally the farmhouse looked exactly the way it told us it should.«

Today, the Basque »caserío« looks nothing like a renovated farmstead in the traditional sense: After having the disruptive mezzanines removed, Chillida succeeded in banishing any sense of oppression and claustrophobia. He also stripped the beam construction and left the masonry unplastered, with these original materials now coexisting with a surprising and engaging openness thanks to a new abundance of space and light. The sculptor had reduced the building to its constructive elements, so that the building itself became a sculpture. Not only this renovated farmhouse and the artistic œuvre preserved within it, but the whole sculpture meadow – the entrance building and the undulating park with its forty sculptures – were designed by Chillida, based on his concept of space. »Leku« is Basque for »location«, »area«. For Chillida, the space, the boundary and the void were central sculptural principles. He therefore saw the Zabalaga farmstead – like his unfinished Tindaya project on the island of Fuerteventura in the Canaries – as a creative work that began with empty space Chillida enlisted Kosme de Barañano, then director of the Instituto Valenciano de

Arte Moderno (IVAM) to create an artistic design for the sculpture park. Barañano summarized the artistic concept thus: »The sculptures are not displayed in chronological order. Even when you start at the building, there is no circular route. The intention is for the whole park to be experienced as an open space, facilitating dialogue between the artworks, which are situated at different levels on the site, and also between the sculptures and the farmhouse. The sculptures' visual relationships change depending on where the viewer is standing. Zabalaga is a visual ensemble of sculptures which continually creates now impressions.«

Eduardo Chillida converted Zabalaga's farmhouse into a two-storey building. The larger iron, alabaster, granite and terracotta sculptures from his final twenty years as a sculptor are collected on the ground floor. The upper storey is divided into three rooms of different sizes, and presents works from the artist's early Paris period together with the first iron sculptures completed by him in Hernani. A further room is dedicated, among other things, to publicly commissioned works. Finally, a more intimate cabinet displaying Chillida's beautiful and quite minimalist engravings and drawings demonstrates that Chillida also tried his hand at other artistic genres.

1. Aerial view of the Chillida-Leku with the farm-house dating from 1543.
2, 3. The sculpture park with the restored farm-house.

4, 5. The ground floor of the farmhouse.
6. The upper floor of the farmhouse.

Rafael Moneo, Centro de Arte y Naturaleza, Fundación Beulas (CDAN), Huesca, 2004

In the northern Spanish region of Aragón, on the access road to Huesca, Rafael Moneo built a small museum to house the work and collection of his friend, the painter José Beulas. Its name, Centro de Arte y Naturaleza, reveals its raison d'être. Aside from the usual exhibitions, it is dedicated to cultural events centring on »art and nature«. In the past few years, international artists like Richard Long, Ulrich Rückriem and Alberto Carneiro have also been invited to come and create sculptures for the whole province, particularly the mountainous northern region, *in situ*. This philosophy inspired Rafael Moneo to create a museum that looks like a huge sculpture from a distance and is matched to its surroundings in colour and form. Moneo modelled the building on neighbouring rock formations that are extensions of the Pyrenees; he also based the cubage of the exhibition hall on the outline of a water-filled ditch. He sank the hall's floor 2.5 m into the ground and gave the concrete outer wall an earthy colour. To help create this colour tone, he included mineral substances in the white cement.

The Madrid architect built his museum in the midst of a wine-growing area, directly next to the house of the two married artists, Beulas and Sarrate. The exhibition buildings also have a park complex and a little amphitheatre where open-air performances are staged. A pre-existing moat that almost completely surrounds the museum gives the Fundación Beulas particular charm. Moneo considered the closeness to the water very important, and built undulating, flowing concrete walls, which he describes as »burst and fragmented cubature«. Beyond this wave-like construction are the large exhibition hall and the temporary exhibition room. Moneo also provided space for exhibitions in the basement. Rafael Moneo's main focus, however, is the large collection room containing paintings and sculptures by Jose Beulas, which is surrounded by concave and convex lines. As so often with Moneo, the lighting system is striking. Two windows do provide visual contact with the outside world, but the interior is evenly lighted by a »sun filter« – a glass ceiling hung from self-supporting truss beams. This artificial lighting system makes the museum space very atmospheric.

It is not only José Beulas' paintings and sculptures that make visiting the Fundación Beulas worthwhile. The collection built up by the artist and his wife María Sarrate includes works by Eduardo Chillida, Juan Gris, Roberto Matta, Jorge Oteiza, Jaume Plensa, Carlos Saura and Bill Viola.

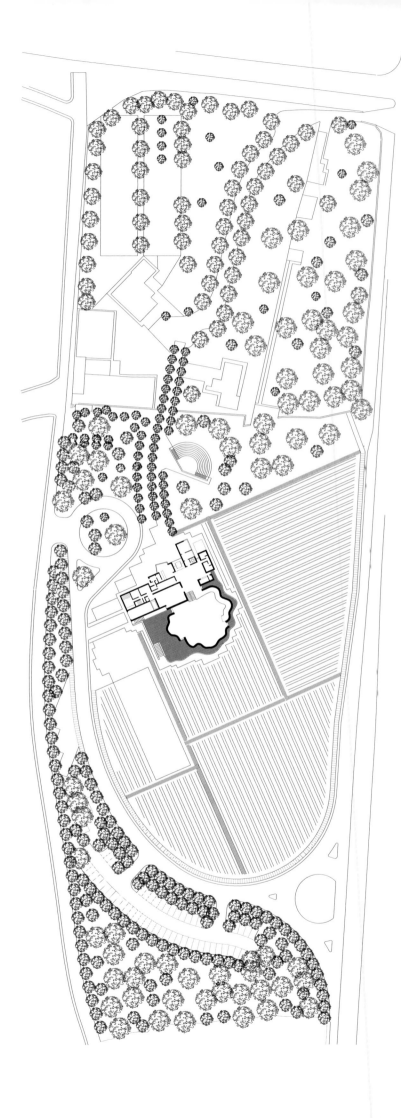

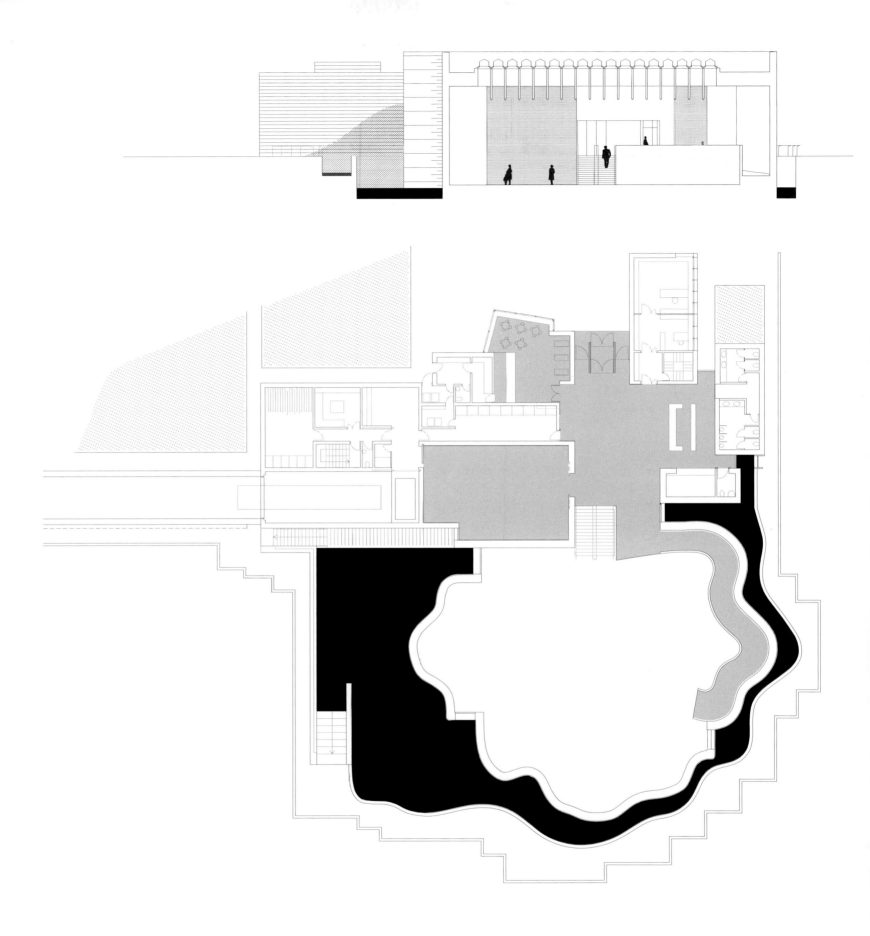

1. Site plan with museum, park and amphitheatre.
2. Section through the museum.
3. Floor plan with foyer and space for permanent
and temporary exhibitions.

pp. 100, 101
4. View of the museum over the neighbouring vineyards.
5. Rear entrance area with cafeteria and offices.
6. Undulating flow of the façade with moat.

7, 8. The exhibition space.

5. Exterior view of the Castillo de la Luz.
6, 7. The interior with a gallery in steel.

Mansilla+Tuñon, Museo de Arte Contemporáneo de Castilla y León (MUSAC), Léon, 2004

In the past few years, there has been an unmistakable push towards modernisation throughout the historic region of Castille and León, a seat of power for medieval kings in the heart of Spain. Iberia's sparsely industrialised problem region, with 1 200 sqkm of territory and two million inhabitants – the lowest population density in Europe – it wishes to diversify from churches, cathedrals and aristocratic palaces. This began some time ago in Valladolid, where a convent building was converted into a museum of contemporary Spanish art (the Museo Patio Herreriano).

Subsequently, a former prison in the traditional university town of Salamanca was converted into the Centro de Arte de Salamanca, a museum specialising in international contemporary art. Naturally Spain's former capital did not want to be left out, and so in 1994 the Madrid studio of Luis Mansilla and Emilio Tuñon was commissioned to build a modern concert hall – the Auditorio de la Ciudad de León, winner of the Premio Nacional de Arquitectura for 2003, on the western side of León. This area, close to the Renaissance convent of San Marcos which now houses a museum, was chosen for the birth of the modern city. The project has been consistently supported by Spain's head of government Luis Rodriguez Zapatero, himself a native of Castile and León. It is therefore not so surprising that the medieval city is to be the site for a conference centre as well. A restricted competition was announced. Out of

a high-calibre field of competitors, Dominique Perrault won with a daring design unveiled at the New York Museum of Modern Art in early 2006 incorporating an old sugar factory and a high-speed rail station into its ensemble.

Thus far, the highlight of the new city district has been the Museo de Arte Contemporáneo de Castilla y León (MUSAC) by Mansilla+Tuñon, awarded the international Mies van der Rohe Award in 2007. This art gallery is situated directly on the Avenida de los Reyes Leones, which leads out of the old city of León. The brilliant colours of the courtyard at its entrance attract visitors in. There is no lack of space in the inhospitable area surrounding the new residential area, allowing the MUSAC an area of 18 000 sqm and 3 400 sqm of exhibition space. An impressive design for the façade, which was to face the teeming main road, was a high priority for the architects. The single-storey modules for exhibitions, studios, administration, auditoria, library, restaurant, cafe and foyer are grouped together in an indented cluster, with the access route via the front court left free in the middle. The façade, which suggests a three-storey ensemble, was designed by Mansilla+Tuñon to be as eye-catching as possible. All 3 351 of the glass mosaics from the rose window on the main aisle of the cathedral were computer-analysed so their colour tones could be applied to the foremost glass façade, which appears to a visitor like an overwhelming sea of colour.

The building's construction principle gradually reveals itself as one traverses the wide vestibule. Rectangular holes in the ceilings create tall light shafts that allow natural light to enter laterally.

These high shafts also rise from public areas like the restaurant, library and exhibition areas. They make the museum's topography look like an undulating sea from the outside. This metaphor of water extends from the building's silhouette to its floor plan. Mansilla+Tuñon's idea of laying out sequences of white concrete rooms in zigzag lines comes from the meandering Río Duero. These rooms flow into one another. Each unit is divided into a square and a rhombus, and each room segment creates different perspectives – of other rooms, of patios, of light shafts, of the front courtyard.

What initially seems like a whimsical approach is in fact based on a rigorous system. A square space follows each rhombus. Even the flooring slabs follow this pattern. Luis Mansilla and Emilio Tuñon are both passionate chess players, and have an interest in this modular sequence because of the surprising combinations it permits. Seeing the results, one realizes that this seriality, also emphasised by the sequence in the five hundred steel-reinforced truss beams beneath the ceiling, continually creates different spatial impressions. Unfortunately, the first exhibitions have shown that it takes a very daring curator to present art well in these wide spaces without compromising their spatial atmosphere.

Founding director Rafael Doctor took on a major commitment with the MUSAC. He considers his »museum for the 21st century« unparalleled in the Spanish art exhibition scene, with few international art centres able to compete. It is certainly remarkable that Spain is (still) able to provide funds for museums and collections from the pub-

lic purse. Behind the MUSAC, for instance, is the regional government of Castilla y León, which annually contributes 5 million euros, 2 million of which goesto accumulating its own collection (by comparison, the two major NRW K20 and K21 art collection buildings in wealthy Dusseldorf receive seven million euros from regional funds). Thanks to these generous public contributions, the MUSAC owns 700 artworks by 200 contemporary artists, including stars like Andreas Gursky, Pipilotti Rist, Candida Höfer, Santiago Sierra, Thomas Hirschhorn and Pilar Albarracín.

Whether the idea works in practice – whether a museum with at least 3 400 sqm of exhibition space is worth León's while and whether tourists will be keen to visit modern-art exhibitions together with the cathedrals, pantheon and basilica – was for a long time debatable. However, a year after its opening the MUSAC had attracted 200 000 visitors – in a city with only 140 000 inhabitants.

1–3. Exterior views.

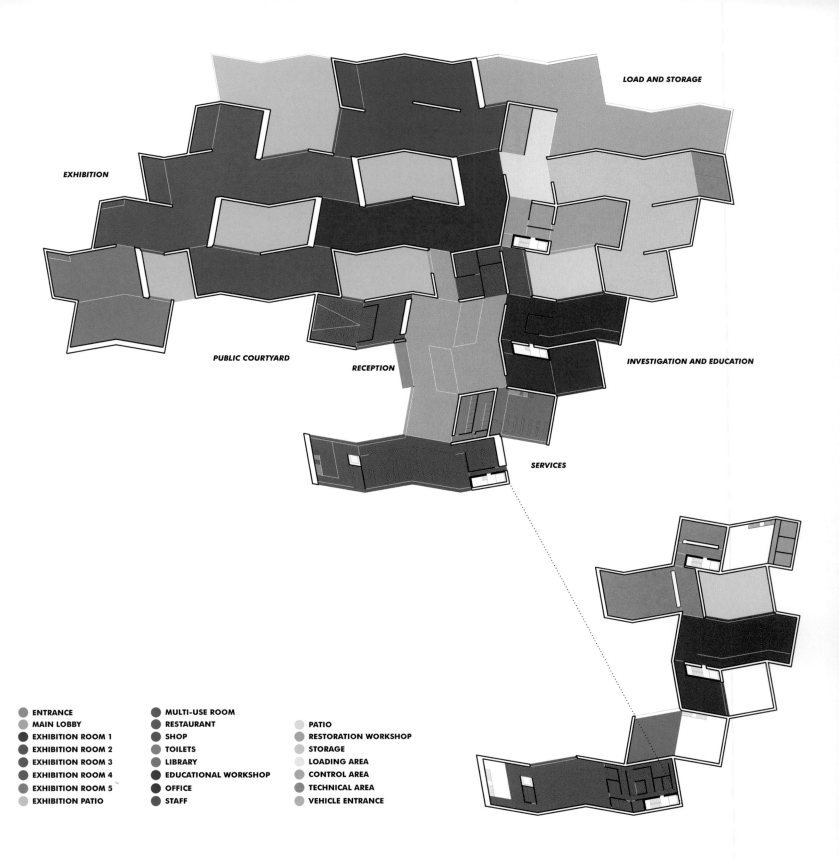

LOAD AND STORAGE

EXHIBITION

PUBLIC COURTYARD

RECEPTION

INVESTIGATION AND EDUCATION

SERVICES

- ● ENTRANCE
- ● MAIN LOBBY
- ● EXHIBITION ROOM 1
- ● EXHIBITION ROOM 2
- ● EXHIBITION ROOM 3
- ● EXHIBITION ROOM 4
- ● EXHIBITION ROOM 5
- ● EXHIBITION PATIO

- ● MULTI-USE ROOM
- ● RESTAURANT
- ● SHOP
- ● TOILETS
- ● LIBRARY
- ● EDUCATIONAL WORKSHOP
- ● OFFICE
- ● STAFF

- ● PATIO
- ● RESTORATION WORKSHOP
- ● STORAGE
- ● LOADING AREA
- ● CONTROL AREA
- ● TECHNICAL AREA
- ● VEHICLE ENTRANCE

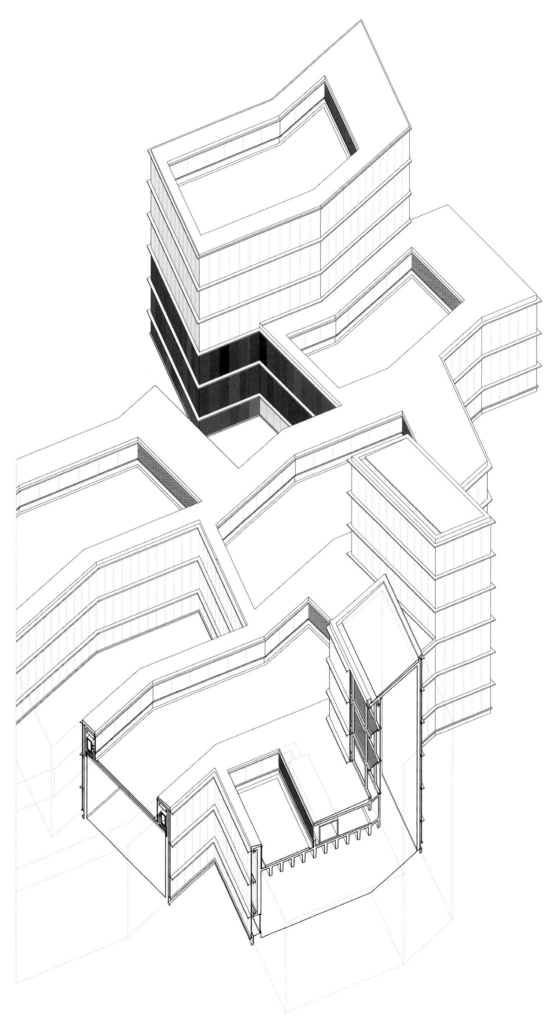

4. Schematic floor plan showing the modular system of the museum.
5. Axonometric drawing of a part of the museum.

6. The foyer with strikingly high light wells.
7, 8. The exhibition space.

Paseo del Arte, Madrid

Madrid's Paseo del Prado is a six lane traffic artery which cars roar through as they head toward Atocha and Plaza de Cibeles. Not, however, for much longer, as the »Paseo del Prado«/»Paseo Recoletos« (and, more recently, »Paseo del Arte«) project aims to recreate »the historic tradition of the site« – as Museo del Prado director Miguel Zugaza puts it. An integral part of this is restoring the original form of the Salón del Prado. The people of Madrid used to stroll along this road, past the Royal Botanical Gardens, the noblemen's palaces, the Palacio del Buen Retiro, the Museo del Prado and expansive green spaces.

It was Carlos III who laid the foundation stone for the public pleasure garden, and also commissioned the best sculptors and landscape architects to create parks, gardens and fountains for the population during the 1760s. One of the most important Salón del Prado buildings, the Prado itself, was built a short time later, initially housing the academy's natural history cabinet. In 1819, this building by the renowned classical architect Juan de Villanueva was used to house the Habsburg king Philip IV's famous collection of paintings, and received the name Museo Nacional del Prado. This exceptional collection had previously been housed in the neighbouring Palacio del Buen Retiro pleasure palace, which made Philip's reputation as a great Spanish Golden Age art patron. The decline and descent into disrepair of this royal palace began in 1808, when Napoleon's soldiers occupied the huge, square-plan Renaissance palace and converted it into a barracks. Only two sections of the Palacio del Buen Retiro remain today: the Salón de los Reinos (today Museo del Ejército) and the classically converted ballroom (or Casón del Buen Retiro) with its ceiling frescoes by Luca Giordano. In 1983, the now rather neglected Casón was the starting point for the heady Spanish museum boom. This was where Picasso's *Guernica* returned to Spain after 42 years of exile spent in New York's Museum of Modern Art, causing the first really spectacular exhibition event in post-Franco Spain to be held in the Casón del Buen Retiro. Over 1.9 million visitors came to view this national treasure, which today is housed in the neighbouring Reina Sofía. Giordano's frescoes, accessible to the public again since 2006 following five years of restoration, can be admired in the Casón today.

Prado director Miguel Zugaza's ambitious goals involve expanding the Prado's existing activities into the areas surrounding the museum district, something Zugaza refers to as a »Campus del Museo del Prado«. He plans to restore the remains of the former Palacio del Buen Retiro complex and connect them with the Museo del Prado.

The wider »Paseo del Arte« project comprises the expansion of Madrid's three major state-owned art collections – the Thyssen-Bornemisza museum with its Heinrich and Carmen Thyssen-Bornemisza collection, the Prado with its royal collection and the Reina Sofía museum with its 20th century modern art. An overall subsidy of 554 million euros was set aside until the end of 2009 for the »Paseo del Arte«. When it is completed, it will incorporate not only these three museums, but also the army museum and the Casón

del Buen Retiro, which will house a study centre affiliated to the Prado. Finally, there are the Royal Botanical Gardens and the new CaixaForum art hall by Herzog & de Meuron, owned by the Catalan la Caixa foundation.

In 2002, Alvaro Siza from Portugal and his Spanish colleague Juan Miguel Hernández de León won the competition to design the boulevard. Siza wants to transform the future »Paseo del Arte« into the Madrid promenade it was in the past, with a green central strip (including more than 2000 new trees) and rest zones for pedestrians with a secondary traffic-calming role. He also wishes to create better connections between the museums, the remaining parts of the Palacio del Buen Retiro and the Botanical Gardens. The »Paseo del Arte« project is also intended to rejuvenate the run-down Lavapiés district, adjacent to the Museo Reina Sofía, through improved cultural activities. Unfortunately the project has been repeatedly blocked over the past few years because Carmen Cervera, the widow of Heinrich Thyssen-Bornemisza, objected to certain old trees on the grounds of the Museo Thyssen-Bornemisza being felled. The baroness also criticized the continued high traffic pressure immediately outside her museum implied by the project. Cervera's supporters have included Isabel Aguirre, president of Madrid's autonomous government.

Site plan. 1 Plaza Cánovas del Castillo, 2 Plaza de Colón, 3 Plaza Cibeles, 4 Plaza del Emperador Carlos V, 5 Real Jardín Botánico de Madrid, 6 Estación de Madrid Atocha, 7 Parco del Retiro, 8 Museo Thyssen, 9 Museo Nacional de Prado, 10 CaixaForum, 11 Museo Reina Sofía.

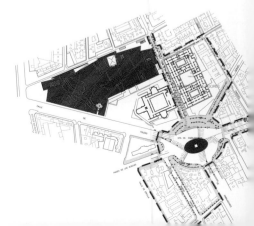

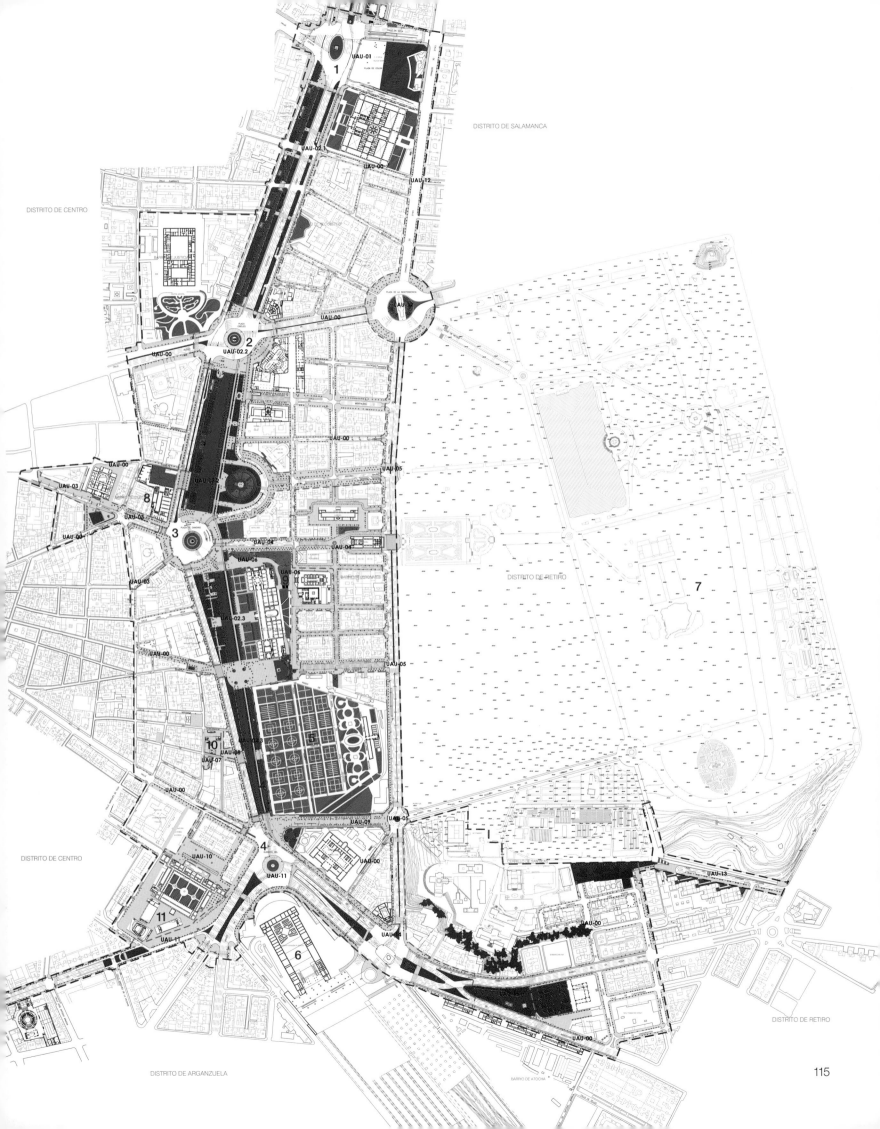

DISTRITO DE SALAMANCA

DISTRITO DE CENTRO

DISTRITO DE RETIRO

DISTRITO DE CENTRO

DISTRITO DE ARGANZUELA

DISTRITO DE RETIRO

BARRIO DE ATOCHA

115

Manuel Baquero, Robert Brufau and Studio BOPBAA, Museo Thyssen-Bornemisza, Madrid, 2004

In the early 1990s, Rafael Moneo renovated the classical Villahermosa Palace on the Paseo del Prado, preparing it to receive Baron Heinrich Thyssen-Bornemisza's impressive collection of paintings. By cutting deeply into the building's inner areas and using zenithal illumination, the Madrid architect created an expansive, airy foyer without changing any part of the exterior. In 2004, the Villahermosa palace was given a modern extension building – made necessary due to the collection accumulated by Carmen Cervera, the Baron's Spanish widow, which it had previously not been possible to exhibit. Manuel Baquero, Robert Brufau and the studio BOPBAA – the winners of the competition – responded to the classical palace, with its monumental gesture, by erecting a transverse block. After creating several very different designs, they had chosen a building volume that emphasized the unity of the new ensemble while allowing the new construction a modern façade design. In front of the extension building is a glazed pavilion housing

the museum's cafe; from here, visitors can look out on a little garden vista extending as far as the Paseo del Prado.

This museum annexe, with its narrow, storey-high windows, has 16 exhibition rooms, organically connected to the old building. The pink-painted walls are the only reminder to the visitor that the paintings in the extension building are from Carmen Cervera's collection. Unlike the late Baron Thyssen-Bornemisza himself, his widow must be particularly drawn to American historical paintings of the 19th century. Some visitors may be surprised to see these genre paintings with an epic character next to European Modernist masterpieces – paintings by van Gogh, Rodin, Monet, Gauguin, Munch, Constable and Beckmann, but also by Goya and Picasso. Most of the new acquisitions were added to complete the collection's stock of 17th century Dutch paintings, of 18th century veduta paintings and, finally, of impressionistic and expressionistic paintings.

Among the impressive museums on the new Paseo del Prado, the Museo Thyssen-Bornemiza can boast the highest growth in visitor numbers. In 2007, 980 000 art devotees visited the museum – 33% more than in the previous year. Guil-

lermo Solana, the museum's head curator, has reacted to this influx of visitors by increasingly putting on shows tailored to smaller, more select circles of art lovers in addition to his highly popular exhibitions featuring Modigliani and Russian avant-garde artists. The museum's collaboration with the fine arts centre of the Fundación Caja Madrid at the Plaza San Martín is also part of this new concept.

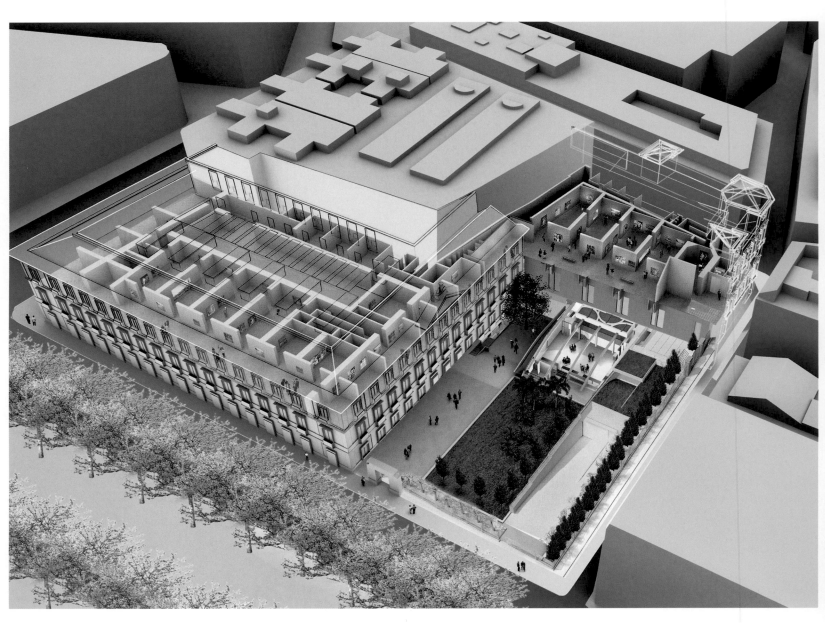

1. Model.
2, 3. Exterior views.

4, 5. Interior views.

Herzog & de Meuron, CaixaForum, Madrid, 2008

Conversion work on the three famous state-run museums on Paseo del Prado concluded in the autumn of 2007 with Rafael Moneo's extension for the Museo del Prado. Finally, in February 2008, these were followed by the renowned la Caixa foundation's private art gallery. Madrid had to wait a long time for the CaixaForum, a much-praised design by the Basel team Herzog & de Meuron, to actually be built. Now, however, one can reach the new art gallery from the Prado simply by crossing the street diagonally. The Museo Thyssen-Bornemisza, another temple to the Muses with a new extension, and the Museo Reina Sofía, with its much-publicised extension by Jean Nouvel, are also close by.

Herzog & de Meuron set themselves the ambitious task of integrating the officially listed perimeter walls of a power station, the Central Eléctrica del Mediodía into the museum building, increasing the space available onsite by a factor of five and achieving iconic status for the resulting architectonic hybrid. This was even harder than what Arata Isozaki accomplished six years earlier in Barcelona when he converted the Modernistic brick buildings of a former textile factory from the year 1911 into the CaixaForum art gallery and added a sunken extension.

Herzog & de Meuron described the new museum as a »magnet« for all Madrid. In contrast with the moderate forms of Rafael Moneo's Prado annexe, the Swiss architects created a true architectonic sensation, setting out to prove that radical contemporary and imaginative architecture could work in a traditional urban environment. They can certainly be said to have succeeded.

Opposite the Royal Botanical Gardens, the CaixaForum rises from the slightly climbing residential district like a mountain massif. The old building was gutted and had its granite foundation literally removed, and it was raised from three to five storeys. Two further storeys were built underground. This radical change to the existing structure makes the building look as if it is floating. The resulting connective space serves as a new public space and an entrance for the CaixaForum culture centre. The prism-shaped entrance area leading upward to the foyer, with its sheet steel cladding, looks like expressionist film architecture.

The roof profile of the new, raised building, with its angles and indentations, is a particularly attractive element of the new Paseo del Prado museum district. Cast iron tiles with a similar colour to the brick roof tiles of the neighbouring houses were applied to the façade. For some years, Herzog & de Meuron have been interested in these hybrid construction elements due to their decorative and textile-like qualities. For the CaixaForum, they used irregularly perforated modules which protect the grafted-on structure like an outer skin. These porous plates enveloping the whole fourth storey are its façade and windows at the same time.

They enclose the inner space, but also allow subdued light into it, creating a pleasant clair-obscur effect.

The Swiss architects use the interior to demonstrate their concept of sensory design. Teardrop-shaped lamps from Herzog & de Meuron's workshop hang in the restaurant. The elegantly curved spiral of the stairwell is a brilliant white. The foyer, with its upward stair, has a surprising rough charm and industrial ambience, characterised by neon lights, steel flooring and bare ventilation pipes. The violet sofas at the edge are equally surprising. The director's room appears claustrophobic at first, until one sees the window slits directly beneath the ceiling. The two underground auditoriums evoke similar feelings. Their walls are covered with a curved, metallic mesh. The two large unsupported exhibition halls, on the other hand, appear plain and neutral. They are fully sealed off from the outside world.

For some years, Herzog & de Meuron have collaborated with fine artists and photographers, and on this occasion, they invited the French botanist and garden artist Patrick Blanc to add touches of landscape architecture to the open court in front of the building, which was previously defaced by a petrol station. Blanc decorated a fireproof wall belonging to one of the buildings that hems the square in with a living wall of plants. 15 000 plants of 250 different species grow on this wall, suspended from a metallic mesh that doubles as an irrigation system. Set next to the botanical gar-

dens, this is certainly a magical sight for passers-by on the Paseo del Prado. The lively front court is also used for sculptural exhibitions, which began in the spring of 2008 when the museum curators exhibited bronze sculptures by the Polish sculptor Igor Mitoraj.

The CaixaForum should provide the neighbouring Museo Reina Sofía with some stiff competition. Both institutions have become established as leading museums of 20th-century art in Spain. The Reina Sofía, which has an exceptional collection of classical modern paintings, is expected to become increasingly open to experimental artistic practices under its new director, Manuel Borja-Villel. The CaixaForum's collection focuses on contemporary art, beginning with the post-war movements represented by Joseph Beuys, Christian Boltanski, Bruce Nauman, Bill Viola, Anselm Kiefer, Gerhard Richter and Georg Baselitz. As with the Reina Sofía, the intention is to stage concert cycles, debates and other events as well as exhibitions. The rivalry between the two institutions may well prove fruitful. The rush of visitors in the spring of 2008 points that way; 70 000 culture enthusiasts visited the new CaixaForum over a single weekend, and the Reina Sofía also received a record number of visitors.

1. The CaixaForum with its forecourt and the wall of plants by Patrick Blanc.
2. The CaixaForum looking towards Lavapiés quarter.

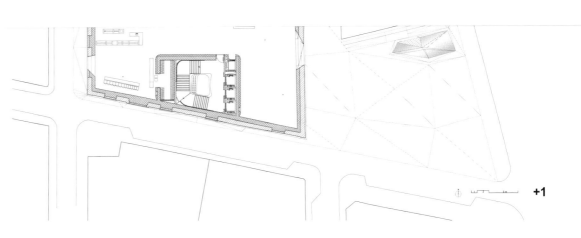

+1

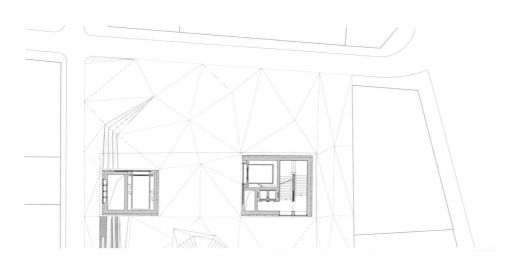

10, 11. The exhibition space on the second floor.

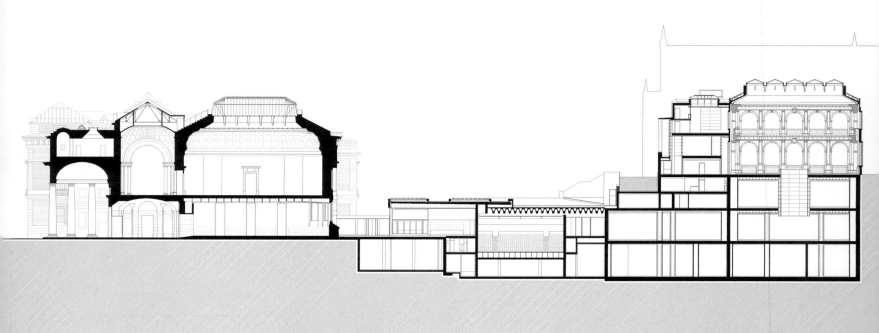

Rafael Moneo, Museo Nacional del Prado, Madrid, 2007

Without a doubt the world-renowned Prado is Madrid's greatest art gallery and Juan de Villanueva's most famous artwork. During Ferdinand VII's reign, it was christened the Real Museo de Pinturas and housed the opulent »royal painting collection« from the destroyed Palacio del Buen Retiro, containing works by Velázquez, Rubens and the Venetian masters, Philip IV's favourite painters. These were ultimately joined by the collections from the Alcázar and the Escorial. Later decades saw expansion of the museum to house new works of art. In 1995, a decision was taken to make more profound changes. A competition between over 500 architects to decide the future of the Museo Nacional del Prado took place. Rafael Moneo won with a very moderate design that nevertheless sparked anger. The Madrid architect was by no means a newcomer. He was already the author of pioneering and well-received projects on the Paseo del Prado; the conversion of the Villahermosa palace to house the valuable art collection belonging to the Baron Thyssen-Bornemisza and the fantastic transformation of the old Atocha Station into a kingdom of tropical plants. None of this, however, did any good. The harmony between Moneo and Madrid's citizens was at an end. Afraid of losing their Valhalla of the arts, local residents went to court to get the project stopped. The dispute held up the construction work for twenty years, but eventually Rafael Moneo's defence of his moderate design was proved right; as he insisted, this design »respects the logic of the museum and its successive extensions«.

Strict competition rules prevented a spectacular design by the Californian Morphosis architects from winning, although this is still regretted by some critics, who point to Herzog & de Meuron's impressive CaixaForum art gallery. Rafael, Moneo, on the other hand, built a very functional building that matches the demands on a modern museum. The Madrid architect was not interested in creating a monument to himself, but in meeting a modern art gallery's requirements. The museum extension, which took five years to complete and cost 152 million euros, provides 16 000 sqm of extra space with its four temporary exhibition halls, auditorium, library, restoration workshop, bookshop and cafeteria. Moneo refrained from trying to make the annexe as a lively contrast to Villanueva's palace. Instead, the brick façades are a restrained foil to the old Prado building and to the district's houses. Leaving the whole front of Spain's temple to the Muses on Paseo del Prado unchanged, Rafael Moneo created a subterranean passage between the rear of the museum and the ruined cloister of the preserved Los Jerónimos convent church. Expansive but not spectacular, this extension was his answer to the lack of space for temporary exhibitions in the Prado, an older building not equipped to function as a modern museum.

Rafael Moneo's extension had the advantage of freeing 25 halls in the old building for the art collection and increasing the functional space by 50%. A new tract with new service areas essential to a modern museum connects the old building with the cubic brick clinker annexe and has its own side entrance. The connection between the underground facilities and the classical Prado is one of Moneo's more noticeable new features. The architect restored the »Sala de las Musas« at the join between the old and new buildings, creating a connecting element for the ensemble as a whole and connecting with the Puerta Velázquez grand doorway onto the Paseo del Prado, as Villanueva had wished.

The new, expansive foyer in the extension contains the cafeteria, the bookshop and an auditorium. The temporary exhibition rooms – the heart of the new building – are all located in the cubic annexe, enclosed by a granite base and a brick façade. In the centre of this cube opposite the Prado Rafael Moneo has put a shaft-like, glazed »atrium impluviatum« that connects the two levels of the exhibition space with the upper cloister of Los Jerónimos and lights the rooms evenly. Transporting muted light from the skylight to the exhibition halls below via the cloister, this quadratic light shaft is a simple but brilliant invention by the architect. Without a doubt the highlight of the extension is the ruins of the Jerónimos cloister. Rafael Moneo had these dismantled and transported stone by stone into the exhibition space, creating an impressive sculpture hall.

The brick clinker annexe makes an effective neighbour to the Renaissance convent. Its façade is decorated by colonnade of cannelured, rectangular pillars on a level with the cloister. Beneath is the mighty bronze portal created by the Spanish artist Cristina Iglesias. She describes it as »a carpet of vegetation«. The finishing touch of Rafael Moneo's Prado extension is a garden complex based on Charles III's classical ideal. Moneo had bushes planted in geometrically ordered rows directly above the new connecting tract – as a clear connection between Villanueva's palace and the modern museum building.

The new exhibition rooms were opened officially in October 2007. At the beginning of 2008, the Prado leadership announced that 2.6 million people had visited the museum in the past year. This was an increase of 23 percent on the previous year, and the best annual figure in the Prado's long history.

1. Section through the existing building (to the left), the newly designed extension building (to the right) and the connecting structure in-between.
2, 3. Aerial views.

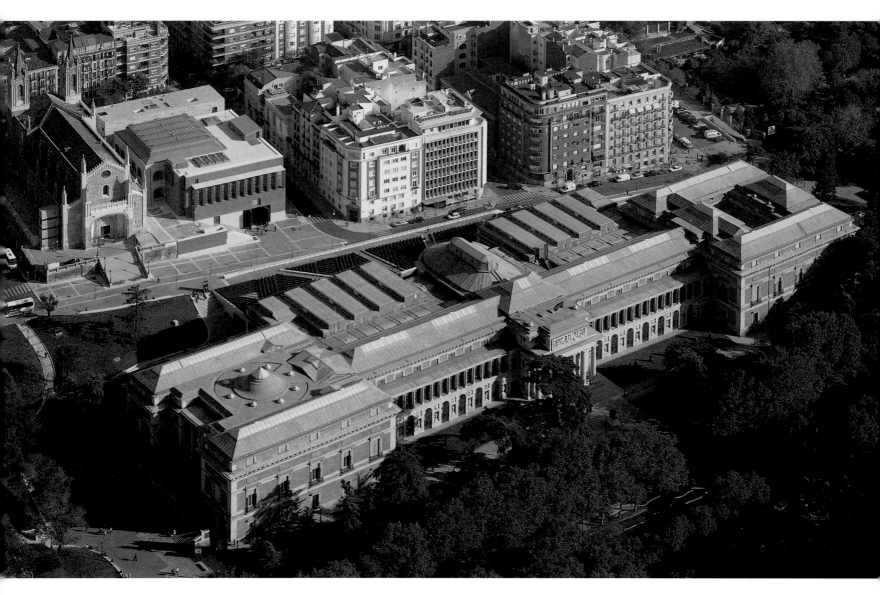

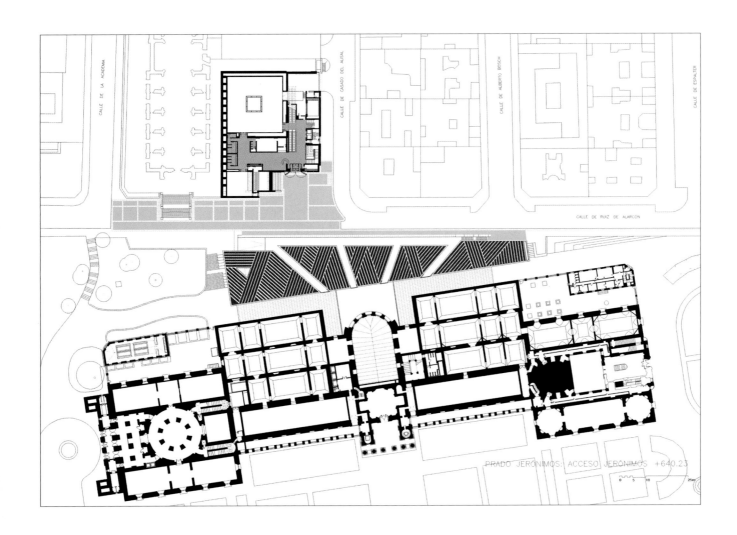

PRADO JERÓNIMOS: ACCESO JERÓNIMOS +640.23

0 5 10 25m

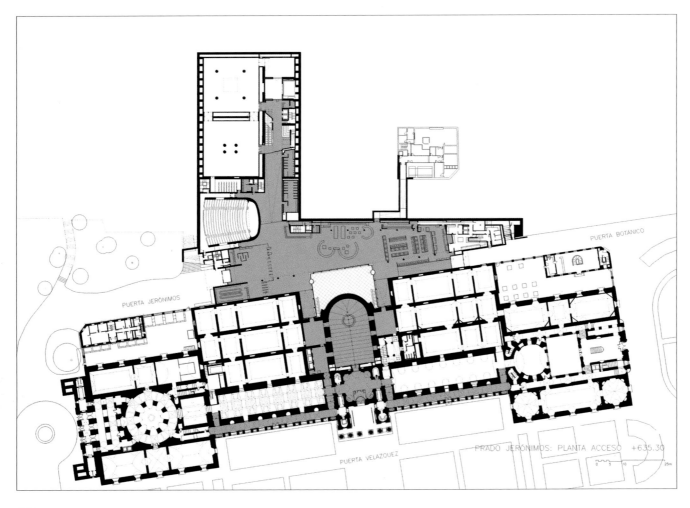

PUERTA BOTÁNICO

PUERTA JERÓNIMOS

PUERTA VELAZQUEZ

PRADO JERÓNIMOS: PLANTA ACCESO +635.30

0 5 10 25m

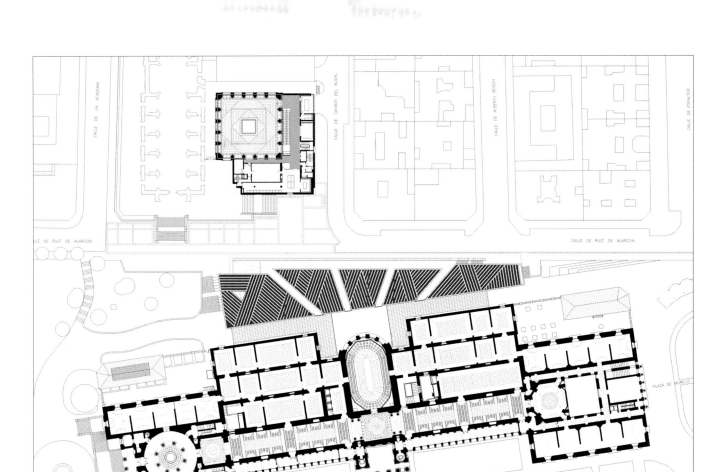

PRADO JERÓNIMOS: PLANTA CLAUSTRO +646.50

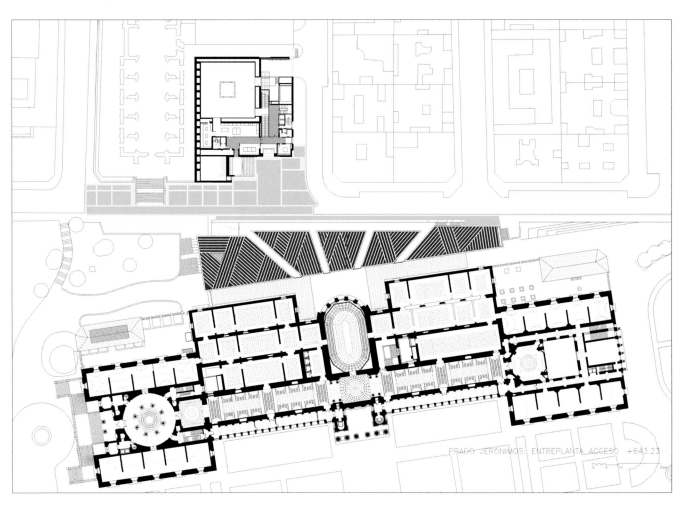

PRADO JERÓNIMOS: ENTREPLANTA ACCESO +643.23

pp. 130, 131
4–7. Floor plans (levels 635.30 m, 640.23 m,
643.23 m, 646.50 m).

8. Detailed view of the new building.
9. General view of the new building and
the monastery church Los Jerónimos.

10. The Sala de las Musas in the old building.
11. The restored cloister as part of the new building.

12. The exhibition hall on the ground floor of the new building with the light dwell bringing natural light from the cloister.
13. Another exhibition space on the ground floor of the new building.

Jean Nouvel, Museo Nacional Centro de Arte Reina Sofía (MNCARS), Madrid, 2005

The south end of the Paseo del Prado, where Rafael Moneo created a magical botanical garden beneath the glazed vault of the old Atocha Station at the beginning of the nineties, has also recently seen the extension of Spain's most important museum of modern art – the Museo Nacional Centro de Arte Reina Sofía, or MNCARS. Jean Nouvel, who defeated Dominique Perrault, Juan Navarro Baldeweg, Antonio Cruz y Antonio Ortiz, Zaha Hadid, Tadao Ando, David Chipperfield, Santiago Calatrava and Enric Miralles y Benedetta Tagliabue in a prestigious competition in 1999, designed the structure from lightweight components and settled it perfectly into the corner on the Ronda de Atocha. Nouvel's plan surpassed those of his competitors where it came to building on this difficult triangular plot and integrating the development into the fabric of the city. In his plan for the design, he wrote: »I propose a restrained approach. Modern architecture can only be successfully fitted into an existing urban environment if it helps to enhance these surroundings while at the same time profiting from them.«

The rearward exhibition annexe connects directly with the Reina Sofía museum and adjoins the former Hospital General del Palacio del Buen Retiro ruins. These stand directly on the Puerta de Atocha at the southern entrance to the city; they were commissioned by Charles III and built by the

Italian architect Francisco Sabatini. Jean Nouvel's building contrasts maximally with the two remaining hospital façades. On the vacant plot, reached via the Ronda de Atocha, he placed an elegant three-part ensemble of a library, an auditorium and halls for temporary exhibitions, choosing a different construction material for each section – steel, granite and glass. The colour scheme is dominated by red, black and grey. The auditorium's red polyester façade and coppery red roof intentionally mimic the surrounding brick roofs. The library's most surprising feature is its suspended glass dome – whose massive surface prevents any disruptive light from entering – while the spaces within the temporary exhibition halls are all differently arranged. Nouvel gave all sections of the extension, even the administrative tract, terraces to lighten the façade construction. These allow a view of the inner courtyard. The most eye-catching part of the whole ensemble, however, is the projecting, almost floating roof complex arching over the whole three-part annexe and its patio. This seemingly weightless perforated copper roof with a reflective aluminium underside is like the flying roof of Nouvel's convention centre in Lucerne. It covers the public atrium, where an expressive sculpture by Roy Lichtenstein is exhibited.

Jean Nouvel brought the »Paseo del Arte« to an impressive conclusion with the annexe to the Reina Sofía museum. To follow the classical ensembles of the Museo Thyssen-Bornemisza and the Mu-

seo del Prado with their modest extensions, Nouvel chose the opposite approach for the Reina Sofía's modern collections, using a clear contemporary formal grammar coupled with a feel for the texture of the city.

The state museums on the Paseo del Prado recorded record numbers of visitors in 2007 and 2008. The Reina Sofía museum was no exception. Since Manuel Borja-Villel left the MACBA in Barcelona for this most important Spanish modern-art museum, the Reina Sofía has had an exceptional increase of visitors – 2.1 million in 2008. Now Borja-Villel wants to make the Reina Sofía a leading international art museum, without resorting to consumerist mass appeal: »The increase in visitors is neither good nor bad. The Prado museum, near us, is focused on tradition, the Thyssen museum less so. The Reina Sofía must therefore become a modern and contemporary art museum that looks at our century's modernity with an eye to the future, thereby synergising with other Spanish and international centres. The increase in visitor numbers must not remain a mere quantitive phenomenon.«

1. General view of the new building from the Ronda de Atocha.
2. The restaurant on the southern end of the building.
3. View from the vestibule into the library.

7, 8. The auditorium.
9. The library with suspended glass cupola.

Richard Gluckman, Museo Picasso, Málaga, 2003

The preparations for the major event that was celebrated in Málaga in the autumn of 2003 with regal pomp and ceremony began long before, and in secret. First, 204 valuable artworks were sent from Paris to Madrid, with the Spanish Guardia Civil acting as an escort. They were then stored in a heavily-guarded barracks in Burgos and a bank safe-deposit box in Madrid. Finally, they reached their destination in Málaga. After 112 years Pablo Picasso (represented by his art) was making a symbolic return to his home town – and taking up residence in the Picasso-Museum in Málaga.

Throughout his interminable exile in France, Picasso dreamed of being able to return to Málaga. As an atheist and sympathizer of the French communists, however, he was *persona non grata* in Spain. Instead, he sent his son Paulo to his home town in 1954 to canvass the interest in a public exhibition of his works in Málaga. However, the stubbornness of the Spanish authorities and Paulo's early death prevented Picasso's dream from coming to fruition. »Degenerate art« – a phrase readily adopted from the National Socialists – was the watchword of the times.

The New York architect Richard Gluckman converted the Palacio de los Duques de la Buenavista, a palace in the Renaissance and mudéjar style, to house the Picasso collection, and also added new buildings. Gluckman, the architect of the Georgia O'Keeffe Museum in Santa Fe (New Mexico) and the Andy Warhol Museum in Pittsburgh, had had previous experience of Picasso and Málaga in the early nineties, when Carmen Giménez, director of the new Picasso-Museums, organized a show – the first Picasso exhibition in Málaga – with the artist's classical period as its theme. For this purpose, Gluckman renovated the halls of the episcopal palace opposite the cathedral. A small but select permanent exhibition of works by the master can still be seen there today. The problems created by the renovation of the Palacio de Buenavista in the Judería were entirely different. As the palace's rooms only had enough space to accommodate the collection, the community had to purchase 18 neighbouring buildings, which, following the official opening, were converted into an auditorium, an archive, a restoration workshop, a library, an office and an educational centre. Six new buildings, an elongated bar with a skylight for temporary exhibitions and some smaller buildings, were added.

In Palacio Buenavista, the symmetrical floor plan design of the Spanish Renaissance architecture dominates, while Moorish influences can predominantly be seen in the decoration and capitals. According to Gluckman, his expansion project was duly »inspired by both the modern orthogonal style and the asymmetrical organization of Moorish architecture«. He successfully integrated the white cubes into the texture of the city, and did the same for the rear connection to Calle de Alcazabilla: our gaze is directed from a small grove of palm trees to the remains of the Roman theatre to the Moorish Alcazaba. Phoenician and Roman remains, which can now be viewed in the museum, were fortuitously discovered during the construction work.

The Picasso collection comes from the inheritance of Paulo's widow Christine Ruiz Picasso and her son Bernard. During the museum's opening, both declared their intention to »gift the artworks to the museum unconditionally and out of generosity«.

Given the accumulation of Picasso museums in Paris, Barcelona and Munster, it makes sense to ask what the collection of the new Picasso museum in Málaga has to offer. Unlike Barcelona's Picasso museum, which focuses on his early period, the new Málaga museum has material from all the phases of his work. The most important pieces include Picasso's disturbing portrait of his dead friend Casagemas (1901), his sensitive image of the young Paolo in a cap (1923), his tender drawing *Minotaure caressant du mufle la main d'une dormeuse* (1933) and *Jacqueline assise* (1954). A few legal problems should be mentioned: of the 240 artworks, most were freely donated, but 49 works are only on loan to the museum for a period of ten years. Forty pictures – including many of the most valuable – must be returned in a year's time.

As regards the new museum's exhibition activities, most of the temporary exhibitions also focus on the city's famous son. Now and then, however, they are dedicated to very different themes. At the beginning of 2008, for instance, there was an interesting show on 50 years of portrait photography entitled: »De lo Humano. Fotografía internacional 1900–1950«.

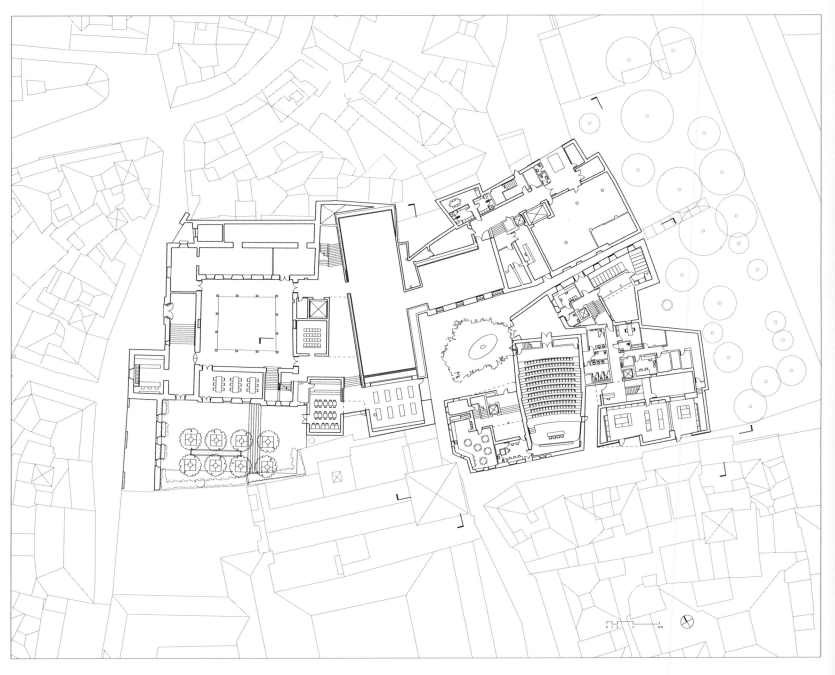

146

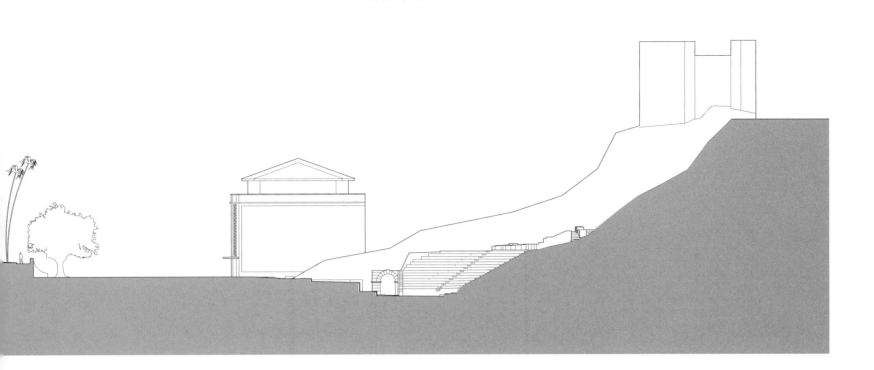

pp. 144, 145
1. The museum complex with the Roman theatre and the harbour.
2. The illuminated ensemble of the museum within its urban context.
3. The patio.

4. Section through the museum, the Roman theatre and the Moorish Alcazaba.
5. Site plan.
6. Section through the main exhibition area.

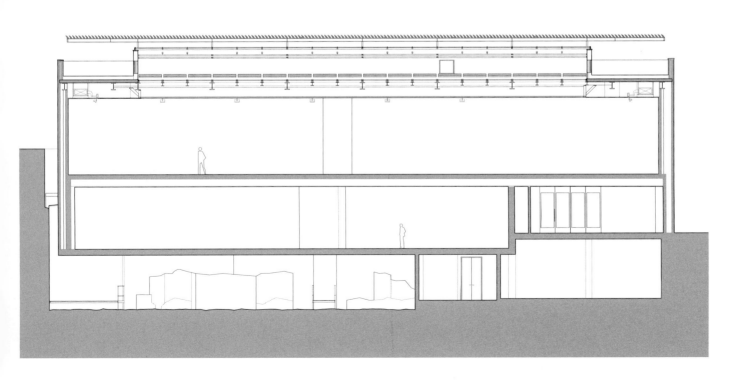

7. The entrance hall.
8. The main exhibition hall.

Wolf Vostell, Museo Vostell Malpartida, Malpartida de Cáceres, 1998

Malpartida de Cáceres in Extremadura is a sleepy backwater. Here the old people can be seen sitting out in the sun in slippers and visored caps at the crack of dawn, waiting for the coming day. A Spanish village like any other – or so a visitor might think if he didn't know that a major avantgarde museum is nearby. Its name –Museo Vostell Malpartida – seems strange to start with. But since its reputation as the greatest Fluxus museum became widespread, this rural region has been quick to adapt to the unfamiliar. Even so, the visitor cannot help feeling that Malpartida's image as an avant-garde centre was rather thrust upon it. This remarkable story begins with the Rhinelander Wolf Vostell's visit to the Prado in 1958, where he fell in love with Francisco de Zurbarán's deeply religious pictures. His search for more paintings by this Baroque-era painter led him to the convent in Guadalupe, which at the time housed an important collection of de Zurbarán's works. Since then, his passion has extended beyond the Extremaduran painter's works to the harsh and bizarre rocky landscape and clear light of Extremadura, and not least to the woman from Guadalupe who has shared his passion with him over the years.

The museum lies about 3 km away from Malpartida de Cáceres, in the *Barruecos* protected natural area. The strange rounded rock formations nearby are what inspired Vostell to build his museum on this spot in 1974. The museum building,

whose form and colour match the external surroundings perfectly, emerges unexpectedly from behind one of these hills. The building has none of the jarring qualities of Fluxus art. Only a car sculpture aimed at the sky like a rocket can be seen from a distance. Apart from this, the visitor's first impression, when he sees grazing donkeys and herds of sheep and cows near the road leading to the museum, is of a peaceful place.

Wolf Vostell deliberately avoided any provocation in this idyllic landscape. The well-tended complex, therefore, was probably more appealing to many Spanish visitors than the artworks themselves. The old building which is now the museum is certainly unique. Sheep's wool was washed here since the 18th century, until this work came to an end. In 1989, the building was listed. A look over the walls to the rear of the museum reveals the landscape in all its characteristic charm. A pond unexpectedly appears, while the stone massifs of the *Barruecos,* a unique breeding ground for white storks, loom in the background. In the middle of this, as if it had always existed there between the rocks, is Vostell's concrete-embedded car. A »rocket« made from aeroplane parts and cars rears up from the courtyard. Its title is strange: *Why did the trial of Christ before Pilate last only two minutes?*

Of course, the museum founded by Wolf Vostell in 1976 is significant not so much for its architectonic design as for the overarching artistic concept, with its successful union of art and nature. Unfortunately, it took a long time for the museum to acquire its present form. There were two peri-

ods of renovation in the nineties, ending in 1998 – the results of which Vostell sadly never lived to see, as he died in the same year. Vostell's museum in provincial Malpartida, however, became one of the most active art centres of Spain's post-Franco era. Between 1977 and 1983, the Fluxus and Happening activist arranged several art days in this idyllic setting, establishing connections with Spanish, Portuguese and Polish artists. Since 1999, there has even been a music festival, the annual »Ciclo de Música Contemporánea«.

The core of the Fluxus museum's collection, which today is looked after by a board of trustees, dates back to 1996. The Italian Gino di Maggio, who organised the 1990 Biennale exhibition »Ubi Fluxus, ibi motus« in Venice, gifted the Vostell museum his extensive Fluxus collection, including 250 works by 31 artists. The permanent exhibition includes musical scores as well as videos, environments, assemblages and objects. Photos of the *Robot Opera* happening by Nam June Paik and Charlotte Moorman (1965), Ben Patterson's arrangement for a holistic acoustic artwork using »arte povera« materials (1960) and Alan Kaprov's *Fluids*, a photographic documentation of slowly melting blocks of ice, all appear in the exhibition. While Vostell's works – the extensive automobile environments, the televisions abandoned to the ravages of decay, the white motorbikes formerly belonging to Franco's personal escort – are housed in a dim, cavern-like wing of the museum, the collection is housed in a bright, almost tranquil tract of the building. This proximity gives a note of tension to certain aspects of the exhibits.

1. The museum complex in the nature protection area of Barruecos.
2, 3. Parts of the restored complex.

pp. 152, 153
4, 5. The former laundry with a collection of Fluxus art.
6, 7. Other exhibition rooms with Fluxus art.

Rafael Moneo, Museo Nacional de Arte Romano, Mérida, 1985

Even the name Mérida provides a hint of its origins in the old Roman city of Emerita Augusta. This city was founded by the Emperor Augustus and was in its day the largest and most important Roman colony on the Iberian Peninsula. Extremadura's second biggest city retains many echoes of the Roman period, such as the bridge over the Río Guadiana, the Arch of Trajan and the Temple of Diana. There is also the theatre and amphitheatre above the river. At the end of the seventies, neighbouring archaeological excavations found extensive remains of houses, roads and parts of a necropolis.

Subsequently, Rafael Moneo received a commission to build a museum dedicated to these finds on the site of the ruins and to connect this site with the theatre and amphitheatre. At the time, the Spanish Pritzker Prize winner was enjoying unprecedented fame thanks to his town hall for Logroño, which had just been completed, and the Madrid Bankinter bank building. Architectural historian Antón Capitel once said that the Museo Nacional de Arte Romano marked, »a turning point in Spanish contemporary architecture«. With his museum building, Rafael Moneo succeeded in creating an impression of Roman life in Mérida without falling into the trap of purely derivative imitation. In the heyday of post-Modernism, the Madrid architect created a building that did more than simply use Roman-age architectural elements as decoration. He was not interested in quoting the ancient canon in the conventional way. Instead, he evoked Roman construction technology to create the appropriate atmosphere for the archaeological objects.

Certainly visitors might feel as if they had been transported to a Roman basilica, but the simple arrangement of the abstract spaces may also remind them of Peter Behrens's and Hans Poelzig's industrial buildings. Antón Capitel perceptively described this complex ancient and modern referential framework as »eclectic Rationalism«.

Rafael Moneo created a continuous space with great parallel walls, interrupted at intervals by arches shaped like the Arch of Trajan. These serial arches are echoed in the buttresses that structure the south façade. Moneo's idea was that the serial arrangement of the massive, transverse arches would be a good way to represent the monumentality of Roman structures, as would the elongated connective space, which looks like the central nave of a Gothic cathedral. The open niches between the arches complete the architectonic concept. These openings, which look like a church's side naves, house the most valuable archaeological treasures. Rafael Moneo stresses that the underlying construction logic is manifested in the parallel arches and the succession of niches, and therefore in the »fiction of a church nave«. Put formally, it manifests itself as the interrelationship of »intervals, proportions and openings«.

Because the two walls erected in parallel are the building's loadbearing structure, they were cast in concrete. This construction, however, remains invisible, as visitors see only the brick cladding. The bricks are super-imposed on the concrete walls as a uniform construction material.

In the crypt that lies below the building, Moneo interrupted the clear and impressive construction with its weighty arches in order not to affect its archaeological value. The course of a Roman road, the ruins of the perimeter walls, several column stumps and the remains of the ancient necropolis played a crucial role in the clear separation of the actual museum and the archaeological site. There is also a rather strange-looking dark and seemingly endless tunnel in the lower storey connecting the crypt with the neighbouring theatre and amphitheatre.

One of the most striking architectural features of Moneo's museum is the zenithal light incidence. This is the least harsh way of providing natural lighting for the exhibited artefacts; due to the inner space's arrangement, the light only falls on the niches. Moneo used zenithal light again for the Fundación Beulas project. Only at the Museo Nacional de Arte Romano's north end are there also lateral windows, which let in natural light in the same impressive way as in the altar space of a cathedral.

The museum's remarkable collection is thematically organised and distributed across several levels. Finds relating to public theatre performances, burial rites, religion and private home life are displayed on the entrance level. A bust of the Emperor Augustus as Pontifex Maximus is surely one of the finest pieces. On the lower gallery level, many different objects relating to everyday life are displayed in glass cases. The second gallery level reveals all the different aspects of life in Emerita Augusta.

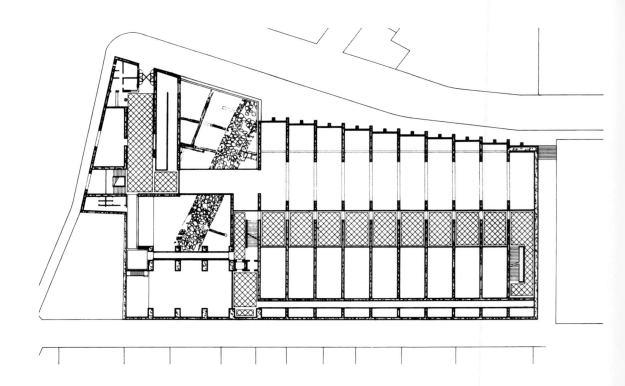

1, 2. Floor plans (entrance floor, upper floor).
3. Sketch by Rafael Moneo.

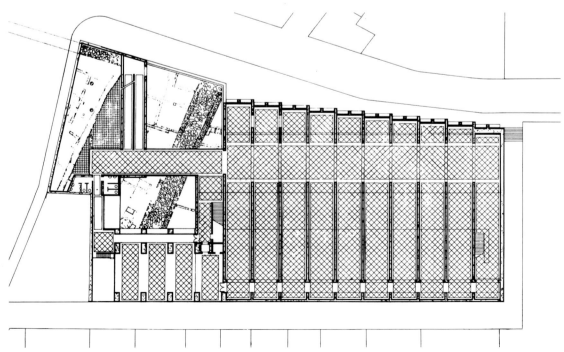

4. General view of the museum with the main
entrance to the right.
5. Axonometric drawing of the museum.

pp. 158, 159
6, 7. The exhibition hall.

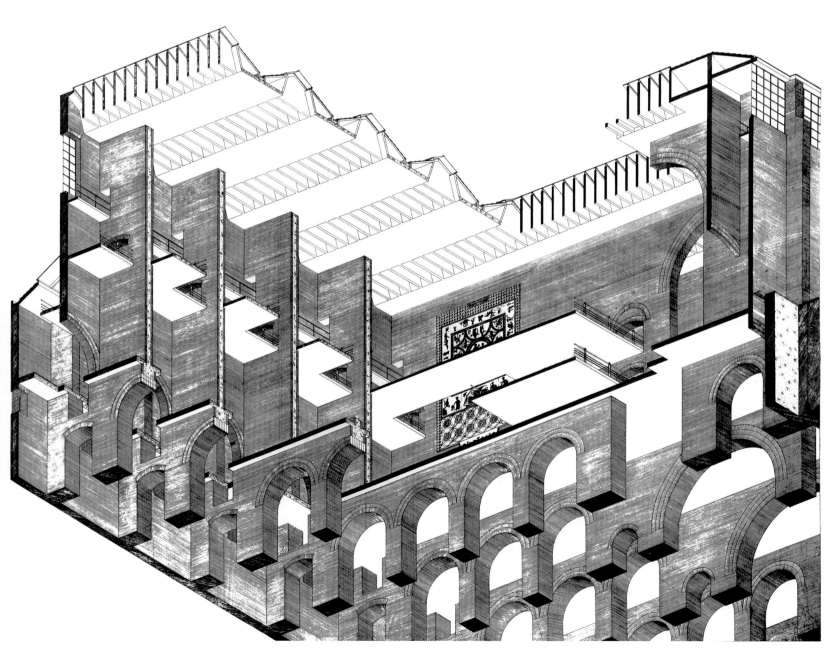

Rafael Moneo, Fundació Pilar i Joan Miró, Palma de Mallorca, 1992

Palma de Mallorca is generally considered a hopelessly tourism-ridden city, but it should not be forgotten that it also has some significant art and cultural centres. Among the most important of these are the Es Baluard museum of modern art, the Palau Solleric, the Fundació La Caixa and the Museu d'Art Espanyol Contemporani der Fundació Joan March. We could also mention the Fundació Bartolomé March sculpture garden and the beautiful Astroc foundation sculpture park overlooking the Bay of Palma. Finally, there is the Fundació Pilar i Joan Miró, built by Madrid architect Rafael Moneo on the city's suburban slopes, with a wonderful view of the sea. Few Mallorca tourists stray into this somewhat out-of-the-way museum. Clearly the word has not got around that the Miró museum is Mallorca's most interesting art centre.

To the side of the new museum, below the Miró villa and the Son Boter studio, the Catalan architect Josep Lluís Sert, a close friend of the artist, built a new studio building in the mid-fifties – a delicate concrete construction with a play of primary colours on its façade. Later, between 1972 and 1975, Sert built the splendid Fundació Joan Miró on Barcelona's Montjuïc hill. In 1953, when Sert began planning the studio building in Palma, he had just been appointed dean of the Graduate School of Design at Harvard – as successor to Walter Gropius. In 1985 Rafael Moneo was appointed to Sert's chair, and in 1991 he was appointed Josep Lluís Sert Professor at the elite American institution. It was, therefore, no coincidence that the Miró foundation chose to commission Moneo to build a museum for Miró's later works on the site that had belonged to Miró and his wife.

Rafael Moneo constructed the new Fundació Pilar i Joan Miró building as a rectilinear, three-storey elongated block adjacent to the studio building. The upper section of the building, which has external concrete slats, houses the library, the seminar rooms, the storage space, the workshops and a hall for temporary exhibitions. The Madrid architect shut the gallery, in the lower level, off from the overdeveloped landscape like a fortress; during his lifetime, Miró was afraid that its »dreadful skyscrapers« would one day »encircle« his land on all sides. Writing about his design, Moneo appeared to take Miró's fears seriously: »Since the fifties, the encroaching private homes and skyscrapers have blocked the view and pressed in on Miró's property. Rather than rearing up to a great height, my museum building will represent a reaction against the surrounding construction. I see the gallery, which is an important part of the building, as a military fortress facing an invading enemy. Its angular and dynamic shape is a sharp answer to the alien buildings which are ruining the beautiful slope.«

Moneo attached a star-shaped, jagged building containing Miró's paintings to the elongated volume. The architect designed this »star hall« as a »discontinuous, fragmented and fractured gallery«. The organic, emphatically non-repeating room sequences certainly reflect the lightness of Miró's œuvre. Moneo used exposed concrete tiles, angled light shafts, subtle views, room dividers and light-permeable alabaster tiles to accentuate the fluid spatial structure.

Rafael Moneo created a *locus amoenus* within a hostile environment. On the gallery roof is a meditative lake area, from which three light shafts look out. A sculptural garden has been laid out in this terrace-like landscape in which almond trees and native plants flourish.

So how does the foundation see the future of the museum? According to statements, it will be »open to the newest concepts and creations of modern art«, but also a »meeting place for authors, artists, musicians (…), an ideal place for thinking and creating«. Far above Palma's bustling tourist scene, this location provides an enclave for artistic exchange.

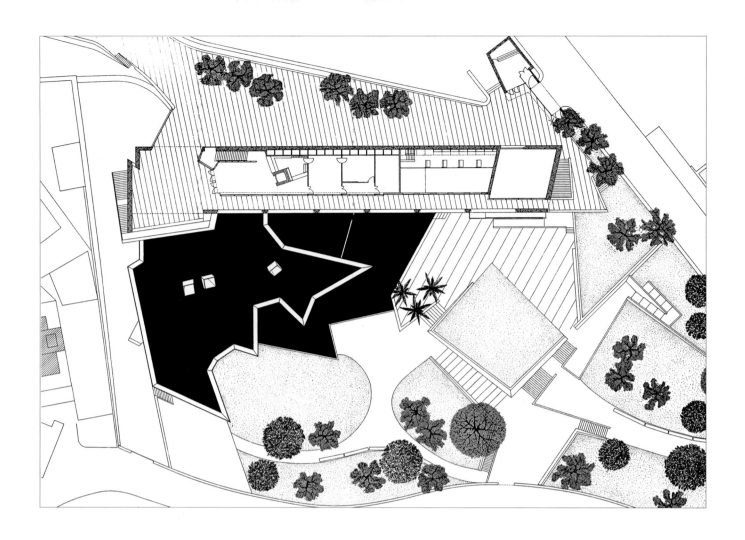

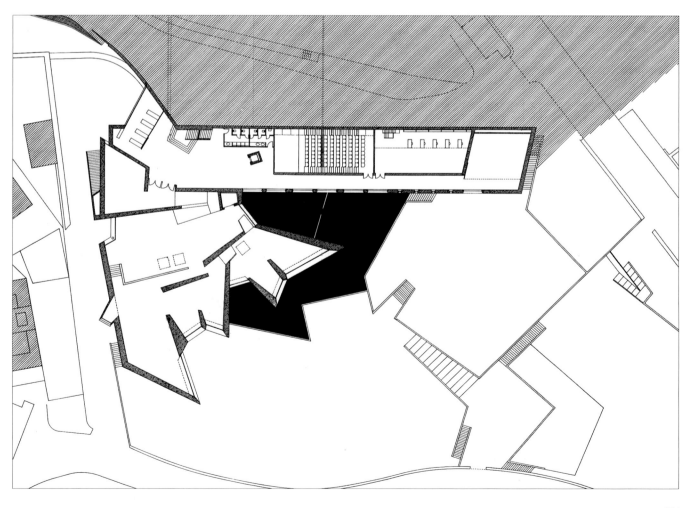

pp. 160, 161
1. The museum in a hillside situation overlooking the bay of Palma de Mallorca.
2, 3. Floor plans (gallery level, entrance level).

4. View of the gallery building from the open walkway in the service wing.
5. The roof of the gallery building was shaped as an artificial pool, from which the museum lightwells jut out.
6. View into the exhibition space.

Herzog & de Meuron, Tenerife Espacio de las Artes (TEA), Santa Cruz de Tenerife, 2008

In recent years, an architecture boom capable of attracting notable architects has reached the tourist island of Tenerife. Among the first of these architects was Santiago Calatrava, who created a gleaming white concert house with a theatrical air on the edge of the harbour area of Santa Cruz de Tenerife, at the harbour's end, in 2003. In 2007, Artengo Menis Pastrana utilised an entirely different architectural language, designing a sports stadium for Santa Cruz inspired by the archaic power of a volcano. Finally, Basel firm Herzog & de Meuron were commissioned to build the culture centre Tenerife Espacio de las Artes – abbreviated to TEA – on a sensitive inner-city site. As the TEA was to be built along the Barranco de Santos, which marks the boundary between the old and new cities, the architects had to be perceptive and aware of the site's needs.

The Swiss architects decided to integrate the structure, which stretches along the length of the Barranco de Santos, into the fabric of the city, thereby accentuating the dividing line between the old and new cities. Anyone crossing the General Serrador Bridge at night cannot help but notice the elongated concrete façade, and may very well be surprised to discover its irregular pixelated structure, with holes here and there that allow a glimpse into the interior. The first building to come into view is the culture centre's library. As visitors approach, they realize the extent to which this facility is structured by artificial light – from lamps created in Herzog & de Meuron's workshop, hung stylishly on glowing glass rods 6 m long. The TEA's magnificent and user-friendly library is active at night as well as in the daytime – anyone is allowed to use this unusual place as a workspace

Built on a sloping site, the Tenerife Espacio de las Artes is screened off by a dark-tinted façade. If you walk along the new street, laid through the building Herzog & de Meuron like a kind of aisle, the picture is very different. The street leads from the mercantile new town past the glazed front sides of the library, down via a projecting ramp to the adjacent Museo de la Naturaleza y el Hombre. In front of the TEA's expansive foyer, this *promenade architecturale*, which runs directly through the library, widens to become a partially roofed-over square. To left and right, this square offers views into the deeper parts of the library. Herzog & de Meuron had previously revealed an interest in integrating buildings into a specially created, public space with their Madrid CaixaForum design. In Santa Cruz, the square's triangular shape is the structuring feature. This geometrical form can be seen referenced in many different ways both in the library's interior and in the building's cubature. This elaborate system of relationships, which obeys a complex geometry, is the sole connection between the new urban space and the freely accessible rooms inside the building.

The courtyard spaces are certainly one of the TEA's most interesting features – one is planted with the vegetation of Tenerife, and the other, which vaguely echoes the triangular floor plan, is laid out as a rockery. In this space, local artist Juan Gopar created a wall with dotted patterns that harmonises well with the pixelated façade. For many library users, this inner courtyard is a potential place for meditation, a *hortus conclusus* adjacent to a unique library, which offers an intelligent interplay of transparencies and reflections, solid masses and perforations, compactness and openness.

TEA director Javier González de Durana's hope is that the new culture centre's art programme will appeal to some of the people that come to use its library. One part of this programme, housed in the

ground storey, is the regional photography centre, which opened in the autumn of 2008 with an exhibition on the photographic and poster art of the Soviet avant-garde. The first floor is reserved for offices and for temporary exhibitions. Among other things, the auditorium on the 2nd floor, with its Black Box appearance, presents film seasons structured around the theme of current exhibitions – for instance, there was a film season to accompany the ambitious »COSMOS. En busca de los orígenes – de Kupka a Kubrik« opening exhibition. The TEA used this exhibition to emphasise its intention to rival Sáenz de Oíza's Centro Atlántico de Arte Moderno (CAAM) in Las Palmas de Gran Canaria in terms of excellence as a museum.

Originally the culture centre was to be called the »Instituto Oscar Domínguez« and showcase the collection of Canadian surrealist Oscar Domínguez along with works from friends of artists such as Imi Knoebel and Jirí Georg Dokoupil. Since the name change to Tenerife Espacio de las Artes and the addition of the public library, this collection, which is housed on the 2nd floor, is only one part of the new centre.

Generally the exhibition rooms were given a restrained design, but it is interesting that some of the wall surfaces have deliberately been left untreated. In these places, the roughness of the pixelated façade is baldly displayed. This of course, can make these spaces, which tend to eclipse any exhibit, unsuitable as museum rooms. We are drawn to look at the construction without really realising how demanding the formwork technology was that created the holes, which have, so to speak, an aleatory arrangement, and are glazed on the outside. The steel framework construction behind the projecting roof on the Avenida San Sebastián is also not obvious.

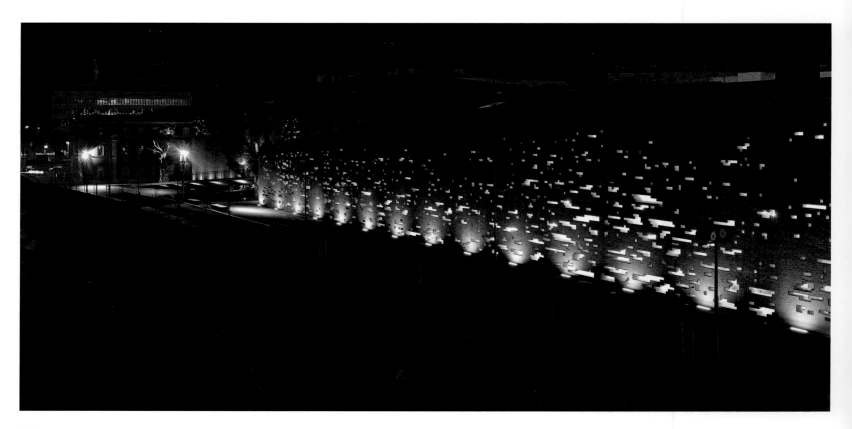

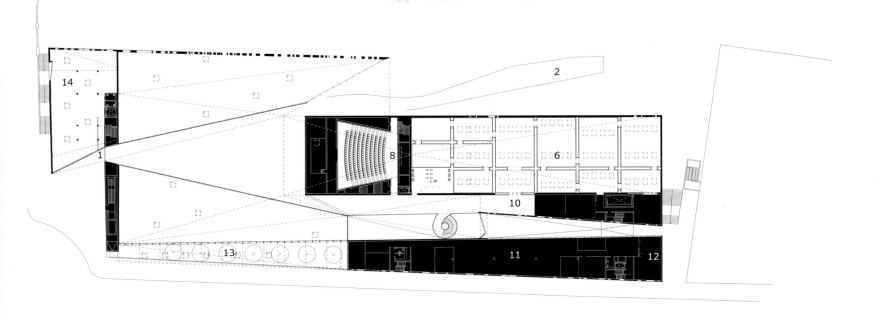

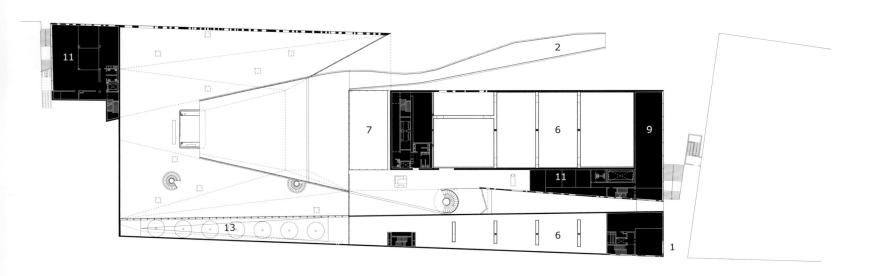

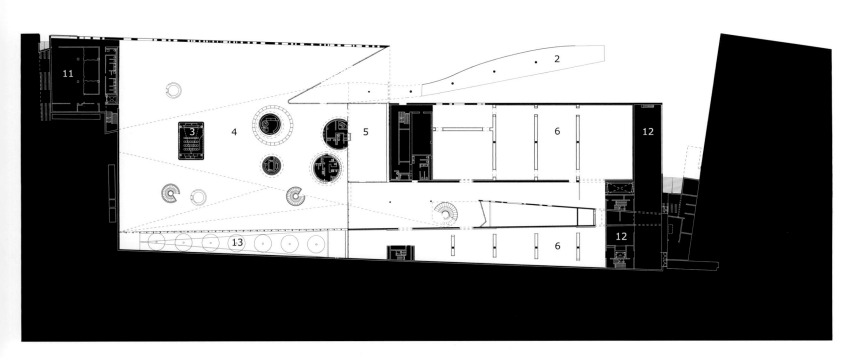

pp. 164, 165
1. Night-time lighting of the museum.
2–4. Floor plans (ground floor, first floor, second floor). 1 entrance, 2 entrance ramp, 3 video, 4 library, 5 café, 6 exhibition, 7 entrance hall, 8 auditorium, 9 design studio, 10 foyer, 11 administration 12 service, 13 court, 14 shop.

5. General view at night with old town and harbour.

6, 7. The entrance ramp with illuminated library.
8. Exhibition hall with translucent pixel façade.

Álvaro Siza Vieira, Centro Galego de Arte Contemporáneo, Santiago de Compostela, 1993

Santiago de Compostela is an old pilgrimage city. To preserve its unique character, no new buildings of any kind are constructed within the old town. Ventures into modern architecture territory are relegated to beyond its surrounding circular road. At the end of the eighties, when the Xunta de Galicia commissioned the Portuguese architect Álvaro Siza Vieira to build a museum of modern art at the edge of the old town, Siza's renovation work on Lisbon's legendary Chiado after the devastating fire of August 1988 was a recent memory. The regional government, however, clearly trusted Alvaro Siza only so far. The museum was to be built next to the imposing convent of Santo Domingo de Bonaval, and they were concerned to preserve its appearance. Siza later revealed that he had been asked to »hide the new museum«. Fortunately Siza was able to resist his clients' idea of building the museum off the road and in the midst of Santo Domingo de Bonaval's gardens. »The museum should not be built as an annexe in the garden. As a part of the city's life, it belongs directly on the road.«

As it turned out, Álvaro Siza was able to carry out two tasks. He also restored the ruined convent garden, based on a design from the 18th century and in collaboration with the landscape architect Isabel Aguirre and the sculptor Eduardo Chillida. Their work respected the garden's ter-

raced layout, allowed surviving walls to remain and incorporated sculptures by Chillida. It takes a second or third look to spot the similarities between the paths in the park and the layout of the museum: »The sloping garden inspired my design for the museum. The garden design influenced the aisles and ground plan of the museum. The building's upward movement matches that of the convent garden, and the angles reflect the garden's geometry.«

The concealed system that gives rise to its compact ensemble means that the route plan of the museum is not immediately obvious. The massive granite building is unexpectedly divided into three nested structures, with the separate sections devoted to the atrium and offices, the auditorium and library and finally to the exhibition halls. Siza decided to divide the building to create clearly structured spaces based on the geometric paths in the convent garden. The elongated foyer, cafe and bookshop fit together so as to leave an atrium, concealed on the ground storey, free in the middle – a second surprise. Rather than create open rooms, Alvaro Siza created sequential rooms that connect across different levels and mid-levels and via unexpected lines of sight. These rooms change continually under the influence of natural and artificial light, which flows in through the lateral openings and the gap created by the suspended ceiling and creates strips of illumination. One example is the impressive clerestory window in the foyer. Like the convent gardens path system, the museum's passages lead ever upward, finally

leading to an open roof terrace with a sculpture garden.

The building's construction hides a further surprise, both concealed and revealed by Siza. In conversation with the author, he acknowledged the influence the Galician and northern Portuguese tradition of using granite in building had had on him. The Galician Centre for Contemporary Art respects this tradition, but the granite slabs of the façade are only 5 cm thick. The outer shell therefore only simulates a massive stone wall. In reality the granite cladding covers a steel framework that is only visible on the façade facing the road and on the portico. At least among Spanish architects, this alternation between tectonic and non-tectonic is unusual, as Spanish architecture usually focuses on tectonic features.

The Centro Galego de Arte Contemporáneo has an extensive art collection which covers the period since the sixties. Initially the focus was on Galician artists, but the collection is now very wide-ranging – the museum has purchased works by Joseph Beuys, Christian Boltanski, Rebecca Horn, Donald Judd and Marie Jo Lafontaine, for instance. In the upper levels, which are reserved for temporary exhibitions, the last few years have seen exhibitions of work by the architect Juan Navarro Baldeweg and the action artist Marina Abramović.

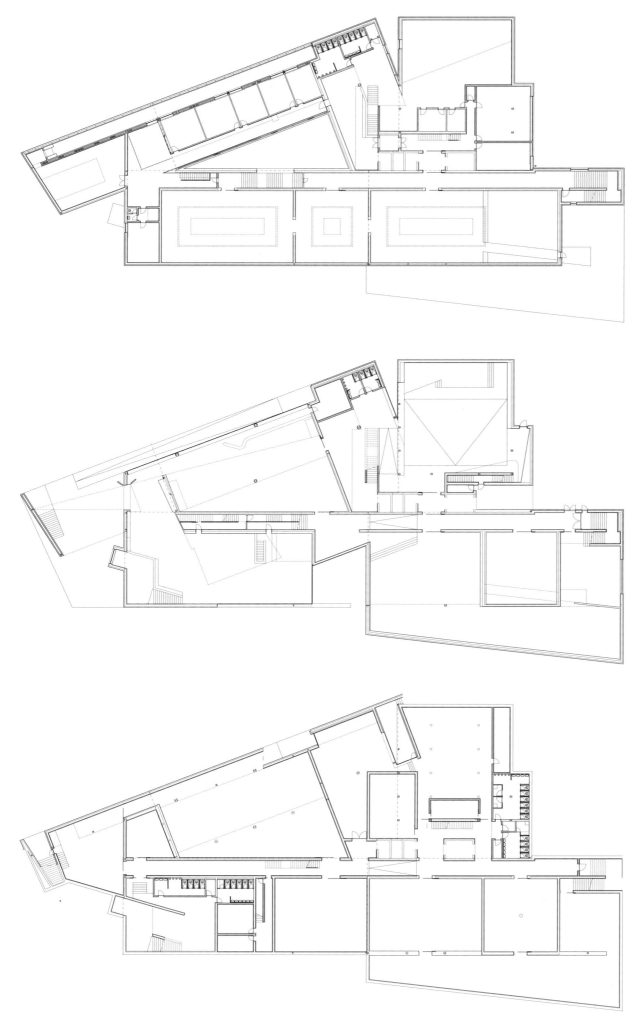

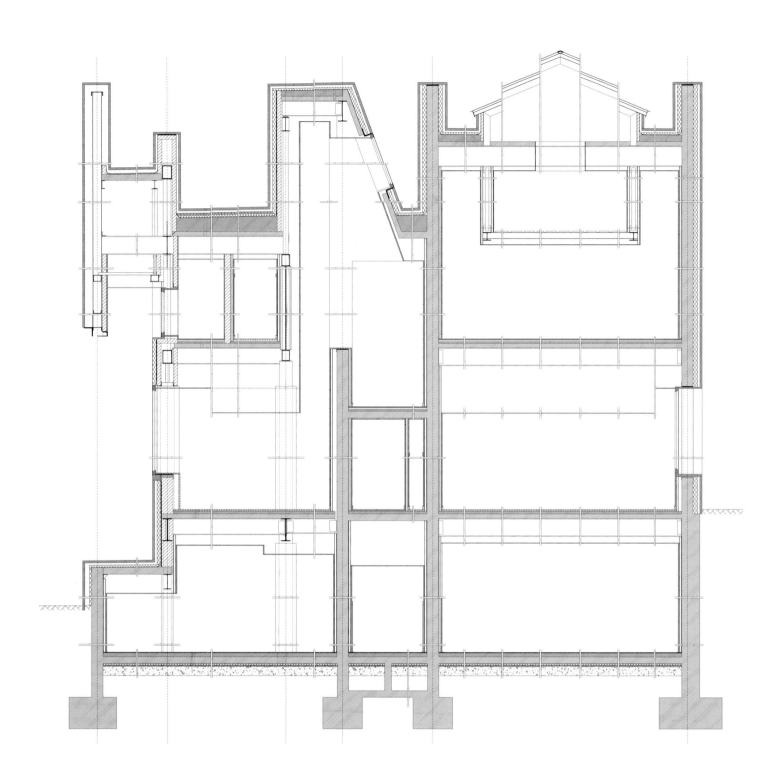

pp. 170, 171

1. General view of the museum with the monastery Santo Domingo de Bonaval in the background.
2. General view of the museum with the monastery to the right.
3. The entrance area.

4–6. Floor plans (basement, ground floor, first floor).
7. Section.

Juan Navarro Baldeweg, Museo de Altamira, Santillana del Mar, 2000

The Madrid architect Juan Navarro Baldeweg certainly has experience with archaeological museums. In early 2001, his design for the »museum of human evolution« in Burgos won a restricted-entry competition, beating Arata Isozaki, Jean Nouvel, Steven Holl and Cruz y Ortiz. It was to be built directly on the archaeological sites at the Atapuerca caves, but party-political manoeuvring prevented construction work from starting until spring 2006. Navarro Baldeweg had better success with another of his buildings; the Altamira museum on the Cantabrian coast near to the resort of Santillana del Mar.

The Altamira cave's 14 000 year-old ancient animal images are a Spanish national treasure that, as a World Heritage site, must be protected. The cave was closed to the public in 1979, as the endless tide of visitors – 166 000 per year – threatened to destroy the drawings. The »Sistine Chapel of the Palaeolithic«, as Altamira is sometimes known, became accessible to the public again in 1982 – but would-be visitors first have to submit a written application and wait two years.

This unfortunate situation was resolved in 1992, when it was decided to recreate the cave on another site. The plan was to accurately reconstruct the cave paintings in a so-called »Neocueva«, with a museum and a cave research centre next to it. Juan Navarro Baldeweg sited this ensemble about a 100 m away from the real Altamira cave. Restorers Matilde Múzquiz and Pedro Saura's reproduced the paintings, largely using natural limestone powder and some polyester resin. The animal pictures were applied on top of this using mineral pigments. This had the great advantage of removing the thirty-month visitors' waiting list, and the carvings and paintings could now be admired free of the traces left by countless tourists.

Juan Navarro's new museum building is also a feast for the eyes: a symbiosis of colour and volume. The terraced form and the façade's subdued ochre tones fit unobtrusively into the hilly landscape. The Madrid architect, who is also a successful painter and sculptor, comments that: »This project has a general atmosphere of hills and caves.« The green roof does give this impression, but so does the way the building fits the hill's angle of ascent. Navarro's building is an *architecture parlante* which, besides the imitation cave, also contains the archaeological museum, a library, a restoration workshop, an administration wing and a café. It is a geological construction. The story of the amateur researcher Marcelino Sanz de Sautuola, who together with his daughter discovered the animal drawings in the cave in 1879, is told in the exhibition rooms. Here in Santillana del Mar, the architect has used a non-corporeal element to make the interior space float – the magic of light. The exhibition areas are structured around continuous »shed« skylights, each 45 m in length, facing north.

The library is a visual experience. It is suffused with measured natural light. The black stone massif of the »Neocueva« can be seen through a glass partition wall, suspended from a multitude of steel cables and looking like a stage set. Navarro Baldeweg set out to achieve this effect rather than make visitors believe they are in the actual cave. His new building bears no relation to the possible »cave Disneyland« objected to by a critic in the Spanish daily paper *El País*. Instead, it is a scene created using architectonic principles.

According to the museum's leadership, Juan Navarro Baldeweg agreed that this »internationally renowned human art treasure« should not be turned into a theme park. Instead, a plan was made to use some neighbouring buildings for temporary exhibitions and to plant the area around the cave with a mixed wood of oak, wild pine, birch, hazelnut bushes, ash, alders, elms, ferns and heather – species that would have been familiar to the palaeolithic artists living here. All in all, an ambitious project to preserve the »Sistine Chapel of the Palaeolithic«.

1. Site plan.
2. The museum adapted to the course of the hills as a »geological tectonic«.

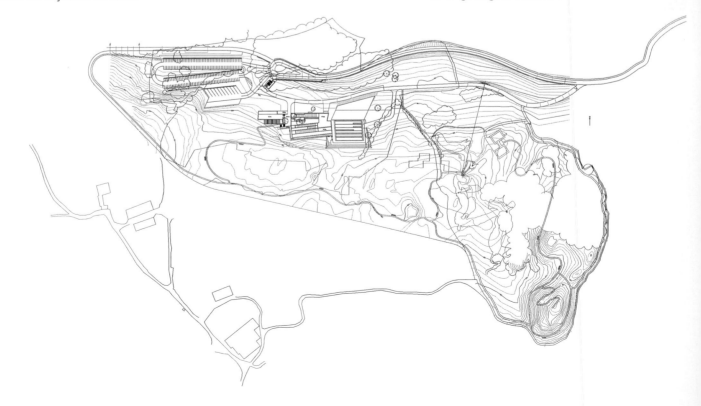

1. General view at night.
2. Detailed view of the façade.

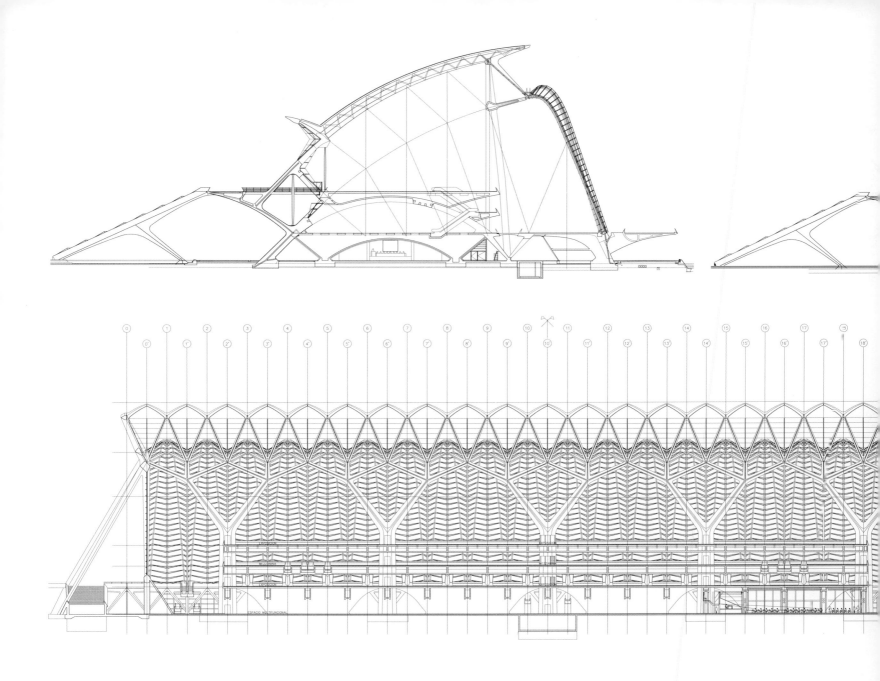

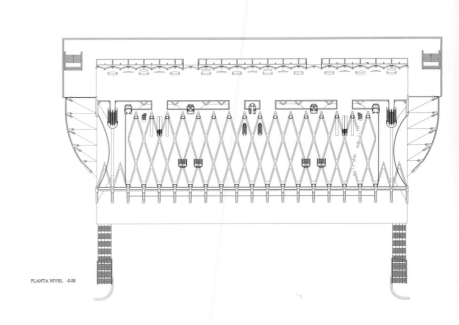

PLANTA NIVEL -0.00

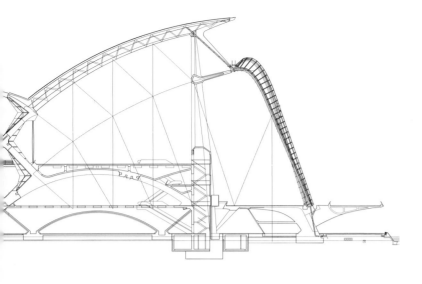

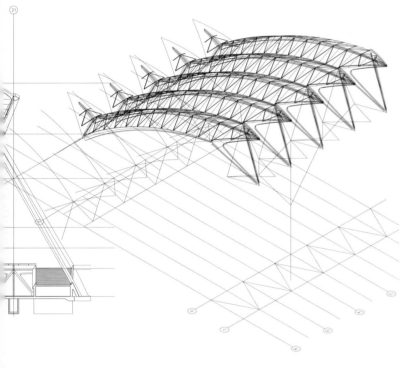

3, 4. Cross sections.
5. Longitudinal section.
6. Axonometric detail of the roof.
7. Floor plans (level 0.00 m, level +5.20 m, level +10.40 m).

pp. 184, 185
10. The access gallery.
11. The exhibition hall.

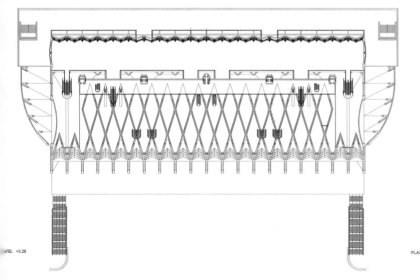

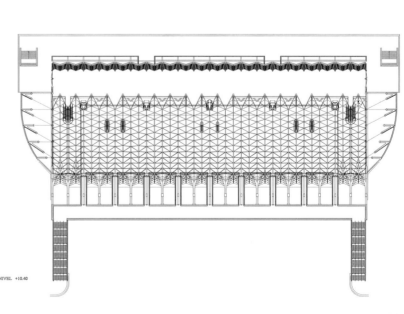

PLANTA NIVEL +10.40

Guillermo Vázquez Consuegra, Museo Valenciano de la Ilustración y de la Modernidad (MUVIM), Valencia, 2001

Three museums have been built in Valencia in the past few years alone – the science museum in the Ciudad de las Artes y las Ciencias, the Instituto Valenciano de Arte Moderno (IVAM), and finally the Museo Valenciano de la Ilustración y de la Modernidad (MUVIM). This last rather awkward name belongs to what is perhaps Valencia's most interesting cultural institution – at least from an architectonic point of view.

In siting the museum on top of the Hospital de los Pobres Inocentes, which was demolished in 1974, where it integrates well with the Guillén de Castro circular road and the neighbouring archaeological garden, Guillermo Vázquez Consuegra, a native of Seville, did an excellent job. Like most Spanish architects, Vázquez Consuegra, who has also built the Museo Nacional de Arqueología Subaquática in Cartagena, espouses an ascetic construction style far removed from the present trend toward sensation. In Valencia he has proved that he can design buildings to fit into an urban context as well as create outstanding constructions. Here, he creates clear forms using a minimal range of materials – exposed concrete, steel, aluminium, glass and natural stone.

The new building is divided into two blocks. One houses the wide, bright entrance hall, the administration rooms and a two-storey research library, which is lighted from above. The second block houses the permanent exhibition. Curved ramps, sloping gently upwards, lead through the themed sections of the museum. A daring bridge between the two blocks provides a dramatic touch. The expressive high point is the foyer, where the space is decorated by streamline-dramps, massive exposed concrete walls and continuous galleries. Asked how such expressiveness could arise in sensible architecture, Vázquez Consuegra answered: »I wanted to explore the potential of every single material. For instance, the combination of the glazed ceiling lights in the reception hall with the Cor Ten steel shows the shine, transparency and fragility of glass to best effect.«

The idea was that the MUVIM would revitalise Valencia's art scene. However, building a third museum alongside the science museum by Santiago Calatrava and the IVAM proved to be a miscalculation. The realization that Valencia has never been a centre of enlightenment came to late. The city can boast only Don Gregorio Mayans y Siscar, who claimed to have corresponded with the great Voltaire. Wondering how best to fill the 8 000 sqm of the site, those responsible summarily gave the museum the title »modern«, which had little effect. The theatrically staged tour of fifteen »black boxes« is best suited to parties of schoolchildren, who are ushered through the series of artworks in pre-arranged trips.

Vázquez Consuegra's architectonic concept, however, remains impressive. He considers it a *promenade architecturale*, a flowing transition to the surrounding stands of trees and the former hospital garden. The garden's palm trees and airy Mediterranean style contrast with the weighty building. The discovery of partial city wall foundations dating from the Arabic period also prompted Vázquez Consuegra to rescue other remains of the convent, chapel and other parts of the hospital and make them part of a civic park.

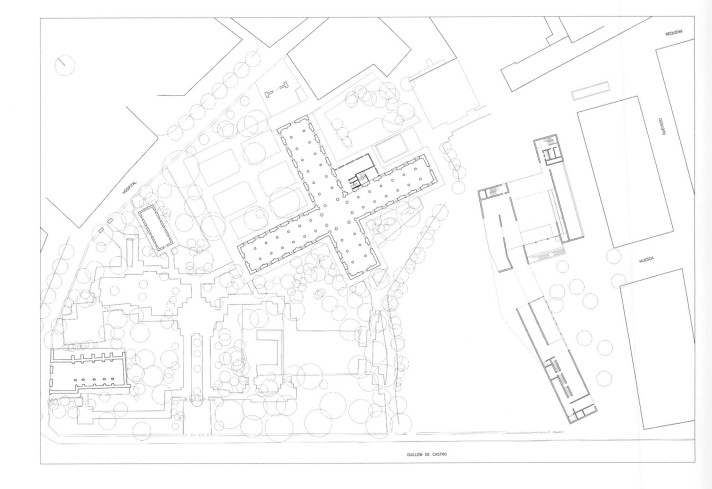

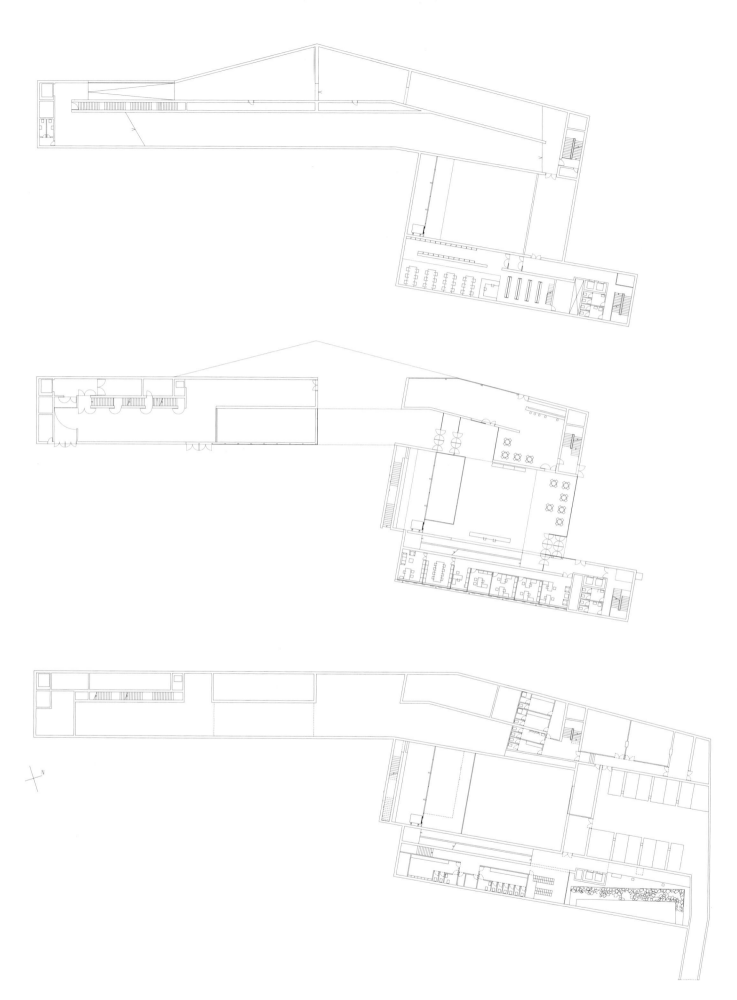

1. Site plan.
2–4. Floor plans (basement, ground floor, first floor).

5. The passage in the centre of the building.
6. The ramp leading from the ground floor to the first floor.
7. Reception hall with pronouncedly articulated glass ceiling lights.

Juan Carlos Arnuncio Clara Aizpún and Javier Blanco, Museo Patio Herreriano de Arte Contemporáneo Español, Valladolid, 2000

Spain has several palaces and monasteries that have been converted into museums over time. Among the first of these was the Baroque Palacio de la Virreina in Barcelona, originally erected by Felipe Manuel d'Amat, viceroy of Peru, in the La Rambla area. After his death, this palace was occupied by his widow, the vicereine Maria Francesca de Fivaller i de Bru. The Picasso museums we know today in Barcelona and Málaga are also renovated stately residences. Museums housed in former monasteries are equally common. Among these is the Capuchin monastery in A Coruña converted into the Museo de Belas Artes by Manuel Gallego. Another example is the impressive Santa María de las Cuevas monastery complex in Seville, which was transformed into the Centro Andaluz de Arte Contemporáneo in 1997. In 2000, parts of the mighty Benedictine monastery in Valladolid were also renovated to serve as exhibition space. The Museo Patio Herreriano has since come to be seen as a prime example of a good conversion of a sacred building. The name comes from Juan de Herrera, the Renaissance master builder who erected the Escorial and the royal Palacio de Aranjuez, although he played no part in the construction of the Benedictine monastery.

The history of the modern Museo Patio Herreriano goes back to the 12th century, when a fortress, the Reales Alcázares, stood on the site. It was part of the defences of the kings of Castilla y León against the Arab forces. After the fortress was abandoned in the 14th century, it was converted into the Benedictine monastery of San Benito. In the late middle ages, this monastery became pre-eminent among the Spanish monastic orders thanks to lavish donations. The newly prosperous monks duly commissioned the architect Juan de Ribero Rada to build a new monastery complex arranged around three cloisters. These areas consisted of the »Patio de la Hospedería« for the monastery's public activities, the »Patio de los Novicios«, which was separated from the public areas by an enclosure, and finally the »Patio Herreriano«, which contained the chapter house, the library, the refectory and the dormitories.

The life of the monastery came to an abrupt end during an invasion by Napoleon's troops, who stored grain and straw in its buildings and took stones to pave roads. In 1835, new decrees led to the monastery of San Benito finally being closed down. After being converted into a municipal administration centre and then into a military complex, the sacred building gradually began to fall into disrepair. After centuries of abuse, the turning point for the building finally came with the Valladolid municipal council's decision to convert the monastic »Patio Herreriano« into a museum of Spanish contemporary art.

The cloister is the central hub of the structure, which has now been excellently restored. This quadratic complex is enclosed by two-storey arcades with massive stone arches. The original building material came from a local quarry, and could only be used with the express permission of Philip II. The »Patio Herreriano« is considered an outstanding example of Spanish Renaissance architecture thanks to its clear and geometrical structure.

The existing building fabric was carefully adapted for exhibition purposes by Juan Carlos Arnuncio, Clara Aizpun und Javier Blanco, the architects responsible for the conversion of the monastery complex, who also built an annexe to house the museum's administration functions to the west. The restoration has left the former sacred buildings is as imposing as ever.

Today, the »Patio Herreriano« houses the Museo de Arte Contemporáneo, whose collection was amassed thanks to the activities of the Asociación Colección Arte Contemporáneo. Founded in 1987, the aim of this initiative is to promote Spanish 20th-century and 21st-century art and provide it with a suitable museum context. However, the collection does also contain works by non-Spanish artists such as Martin Kippenberger and Wolf Vostell. The temporary exhibitions, however, focus exclusively on the Spanish art trends of the 20th and 21st century. The »Colección Arte Contemporáneo« contains sculptures and paintings by Miguel Barceló, Eduardo Chillida, Salvador Dalí, Cristina Iglesias, Wifredo Lam, Manuel Millares, Jorge Oteiza, Jaume Plensa, Antonio Saura, Antoni Tàpies and Joaquín Torres-García.

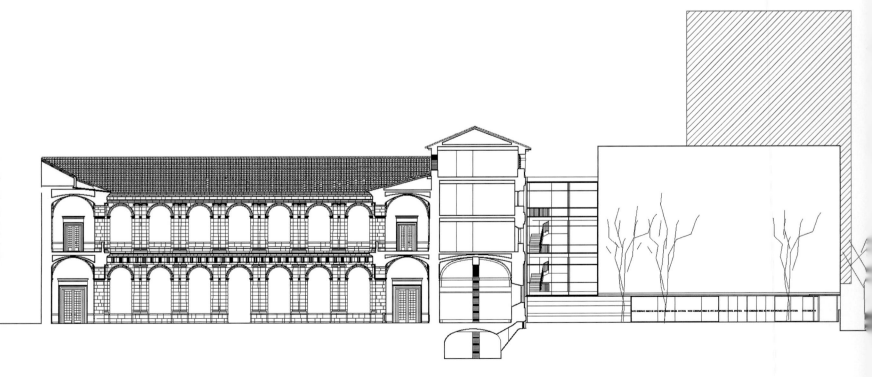

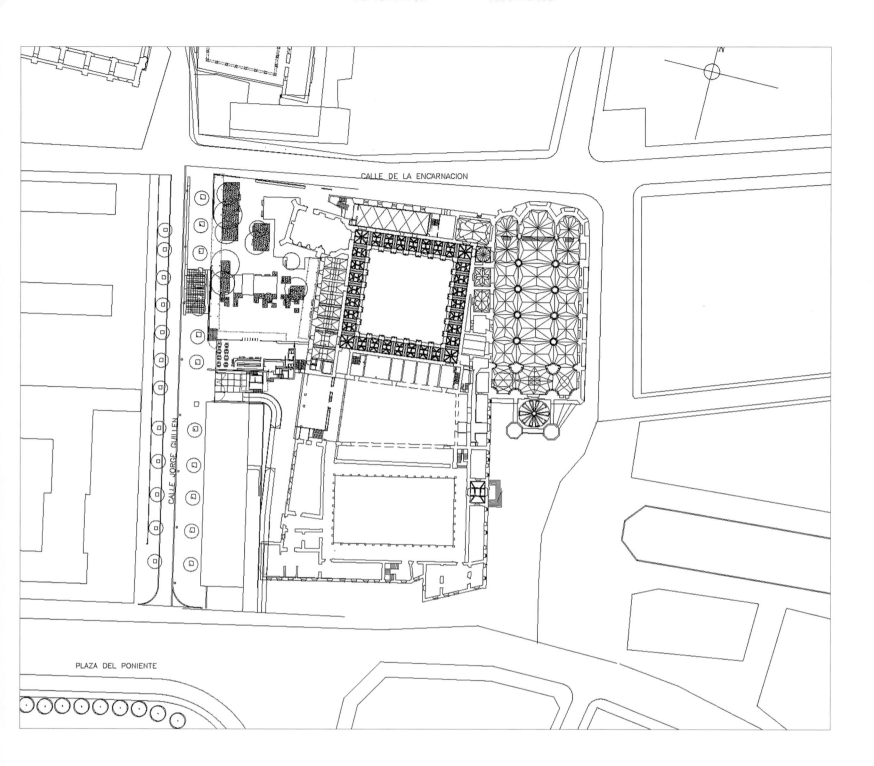

CALLE DE LA ENCARNACION

CALLE JORGE GUILLEN

PLAZA DEL PONIENTE

1. Elevation of the northern façade.
2. Site plan.

3. The entrance area of the museum.
4. The former monastery yard forms the centre of the museum.
5. The covered walk around the monastery yard with view into an exhibition hall.

Aldo Rossi, Museo do Mar de Galicia, Vigo, 2002

The Italian Aldo Rossi's museum in Vigo in Galicia, one of his most beautiful buildings, was created after his death. In 1992, he and his Spanish partner César Portela were commissioned to convert a slaughterhouse south of Vigo into a maritime museum. The Museo do Mar de Galicia, which stands on a former quay, has as powerful an atmosphere as any cultural centre built in Spain in the past few years. This aura is thanks to its closeness to the Rías Bajas, the preserved lighthouse, the moored fishing boats and the fishermen who live here. The aim was to preserve the location's »authentic« ambience.

When Aldo Rossi died in 1997, César Portela continued the project alone, using the existing design drafts. Portela belonged to the same generation as Manuel Gallegos – both came from Galicia and embarked on projects, mainly within their own region, that connected with their locations' history and with local building tradition. The Museo do Mar de Galicia comprises the renovated old building, with five bays, and a new building, which largely matches the cubature of the original slaughterhouse. Another, smaller new building has been added to the ensemble on the quay. It directly adjoins the lighthouse, and its surface already shows the Atlantic climate's ravages.

Rossi's uncompromising rationalism seems ideally suited to creating an architecture that looks tailor-made for this site. The archaic-looking volumes and the maritime ambience create a timeless picture. Rossi/Portela avoided any departure from the old building's construction, keeping to the previously existing cubature and using granite, a common local building material. And yet the two new buildings also have decidedly modern features – sharply defined forms and small arrow-slit windows. Rossi's »minimalist« signature style can also be seen in the restored doors and windows of the old building – particularly in the glazed bridge between the renovated and new buildings, but also in the wide glazed front of the new building, which gives visitors a view of a small archaeological excavation site.

A tavern, whose squared-off stones are extended by a slanting wooden extension standing on rectangular granite pillars, adds a well-judged dab of colour to the museum's grey atmosphere. The lower part of the tavern is painted a light blue, while the windowframes are red.

The impressive plan for Rossi's Alcambre Museo do Mar owes much to urban planning. With its successful conversion of the pre-existing building, it achieves a harmony between old and new buildings – quite apart from its function as a museum. It also provides exceptionally well-designed new public paths and open areas. The maritime museum sits well with Vigo's new marine promenade, built by Guillermo Vázquez Consuegra in the late nineties to reconnect the old harbour town with the sea. Above all, the rationalist Aldo Rossi succeeded in integrating this strictly geometrical architecture into the natural surroundings as if it had always been here.

The aim of the exhibition policy for the Museo do Mar de Galicia was to spotlight Vigo's connection to the sea, which reaches back to the 16th century. The museum also covers the role of fishing in world cultures and the marine ecosystem. In 2006, the museum began a conversion to include a documentation centre, and to accommodate temporary exhibitions, educational presentations, courses and conferences.

1. Site plan. 1 security, 2 main entrance, 3 parking, 4 temporary exhibition, 5 reception, 6 shop, 7 auditorium, 8 coffee shop, 9 square, 10 archaelogical remains, 11 permanent exhibition, 12 court yard, 13 fisherman tavern, 14 aquarium, 15 pier, 16 light house .
2. Axonometric drawing.

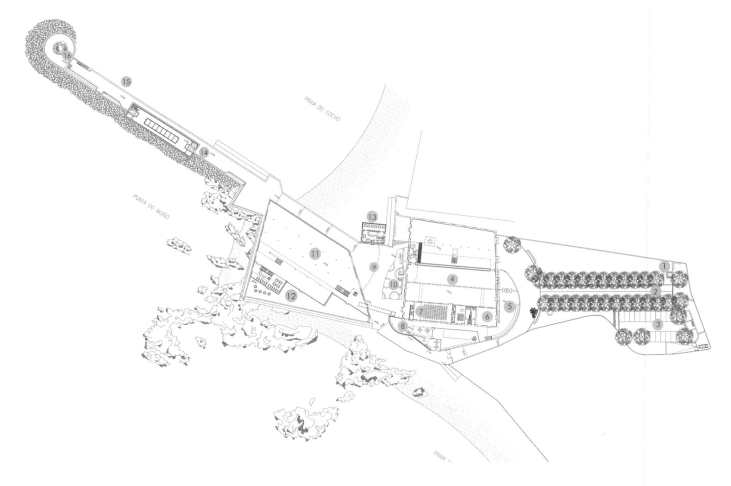

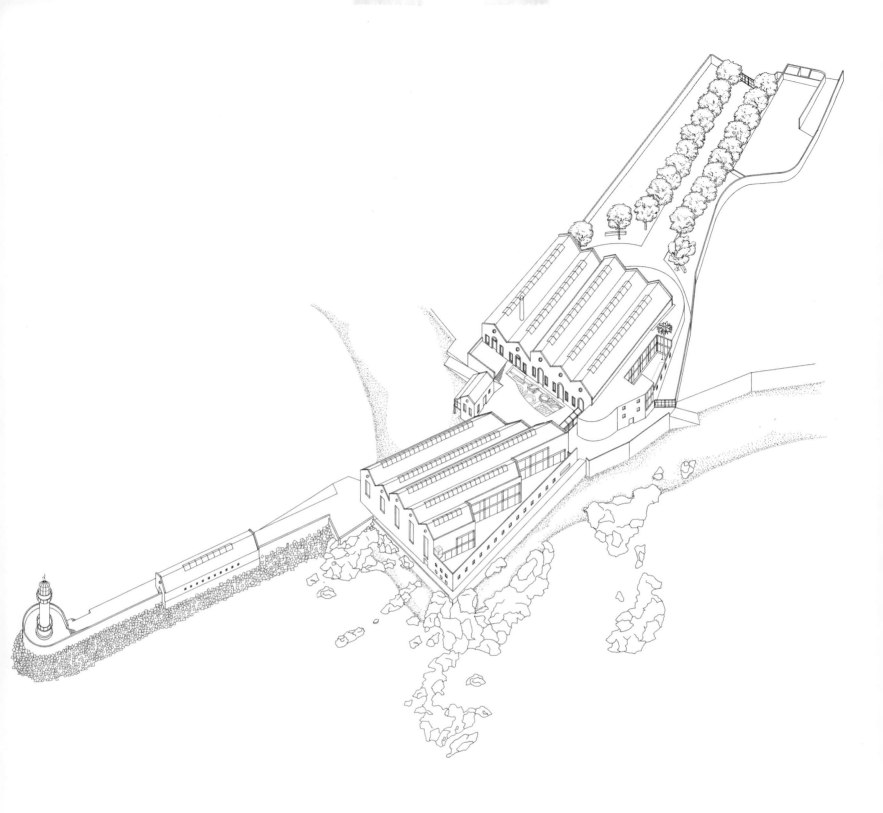

3. The museum ensemble at night.
4. The museum still exudes the original atmosphere.
5. Pier and the Ría de Vigo.

6. Entrance area.
7. Aquarium.
8. Auditorium.

Illustration credits